Chartered Institute for Securities & Investment Level 3 Investment Operations Certificate

STUDY TEXT
Principles of UK Financial Regulation

Syllabus version 12

In this edition

- A **user-friendly format** for easy navigation
- **Exam tips** to put you on the right track
- **Fully updated material**, covering all **syllabus changes**
- A **Test your Knowledge** quiz at the end of each chapter
- A full **Index**

Published April 2013

ISBN 978 1 4453 7276 1
eISBN 978 1 4727 0162 6

British Library Cataloguing-in-Publication Data
A catalogue record for this book
is available from the British Library

Published by

BPP Learning Media Ltd
BPP House, Aldine Place
London W12 8AA

www.bpp.com/learningmedia

Printed in the United Kingdom by Ricoh

Ricoh House,
Ullswater Crescent,
Coulsdon, CR5 2HR

Your learning materials, published by BPP Learning Media Ltd, are printed on paper sourced from sustainable, managed forests.

© BPP Learning Media Ltd

All our rights reserved. No part of this publication may be reproduced, stored in a retrieval system or transmitted, in any form or by any means, electronic, mechanical, photocopying, recording or otherwise, without the prior written permission of BPP Learning Media Ltd. The descriptions, examples and calculations shown in this publication are for educational purposes only. No liability can be accepted by BPP Learning Media Ltd for their use in any circumstances connected with actual trading activity or otherwise. Readers should seek specific advice for specific situations.

A note about copyright

Dear Customer

What does the little © mean and why does it matter? Your market-leading BPP books, course materials and e-learning materials do not write and update themselves. People write them: on their own behalf or as employees of an organisation that invests in this activity. Copyright law protects their livelihoods. It does so by creating rights over the use of the content.

Breach of copyright is a form of theft – as well being a criminal offence in some jurisdictions, it is potentially a serious breach of professional ethics.

With current technology, things might seem a bit hazy but, basically, without the express permission of BPP Learning Media:

- Photocopying our materials is a breach of copyright
- Scanning, ripcasting or conversion of our digital materials into different file formats, uploading them to facebook or e-mailing them to your friends is a breach of copyright

You can, of course, sell your books, in the form in which you have bought them – once you have finished with them. (Is this fair to your fellow students? We update for a reason.)

And what about outside the UK? BPP Learning Media strives to make our materials available at prices students can afford by local printing arrangements, pricing policies and partnerships which are clearly listed on our website. A tiny minority ignore this and indulge in criminal activity by illegally photocopying our material or supporting organisations that do. If they act illegally and unethically in one area, can you really trust them?

Contents

Chapter 1 The Regulatory Environment	Page 1
Chapter 2 The Financial Services and Markets Act 2000	Page 37
Chapter 3 Associated Legislation and Regulation	Page 73
Chapter 4 FCA Conduct of Business and Client Assets Sourcebooks	Page 119
Index	Page 165

1 The Regulatory Environment

INTRODUCTION

The Financial Services Authority (FSA) was set up as the overall regulator for the UK financial services industry in 2001, with the FSA Handbook being the main source for the rules that must be followed. In recent years, moves from 'rules-based' regulation to 'principles-based' regulation have been intended to lead to a reduction in the volume of detailed rules. Since the late 2000s financial crisis, the regulator has been taking a more 'intrusive' approach to supervising firms.

In 2013, there will be a re-structuring of the system of UK financial services regulation, with the FSA being replaced by two bodies: the Financial Conduct Authority (FCA) and the Prudential Regulation Authority (PRA), each with their own Handbook of rules.

The Chartered Institute for Securities and Investment (CISI) is a widely respected professional body within the industry. In this chapter, as well as outlining the regulatory system, we cover the CISI's Professional Code of Conduct.

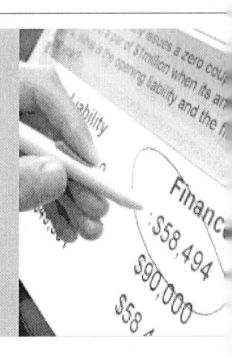

CHAPTER CONTENTS

	Page
1 The New Regulatory Structure	3
2 Principles for Businesses	14
3 Statements of Principle for Approved Persons	17
4 CISI's Code of Conduct	20
5 Senior Management Responsibilities	22
6 Regulatory Infrastructure	26
7 The FCA and PRA Handbooks	29
Chapter Roundup	32
Test Your Knowledge	33

Learning Objectives

The role of the FCA and PRA

- **Know** FCA's and PRA's statutory objectives and rule making powers in respect of authorisation, supervision, enforcement, sanctions and disciplinary action
- **Understand** the Principles for Businesses and the requirement to act honestly, fairly and professionally and to treat customers fairly
- **Know** the Statements of Principle 1 to 4 and Code of Practice for approved persons for all approved person functions
- **Know** the Statements of Principle 5 to 7 and Code of Practice for approved persons in respect of significant influence functions
- **Know** the Chartered Institute for Securities and Investment's Code of Conduct
- **Understand** the rules regarding Senior Management Arrangements, Systems and Controls for both common platform firms and non-MiFID firms
- **Know** the FCA's and PRA's supervisory approach to regulation

The regulatory structure

- **Know** the wider structure of UK financial regulation including the responsibilities of the main regulating bodies and the relationship between them:
- **Market regulators**: The Bank of England, HM Treasury, the Financial Conduct Authority and the Prudential Regulation Authority
- **Other regulators**: The UK Competition Commission, The Office of Fair Trading, The Information Commissioner and The Pensions Regulator
- **The relationships and coordination between**: Financial Conduct Authority, Prudential Regulation Authority, Financial Ombudsman Scheme (FOS), Financial Services Compensation Scheme (FSCS), Financial Policy Committee, Upper Tribunal (Tax and Chancery)

1 THE NEW REGULATORY STRUCTURE

Learning Objectives

Know the FCA's and PRA's statutory objectives and rule making powers in respect of authorisation, supervision, enforcement, sanctions and disciplinary action

Know the FCA's and PRA's supervisory approach to regulation

Market regulators: The Bank of England, HM Treasury, the Financial Conduct Authority and the Prudential Regulation Authority

1.1 Development of the UK regulatory system

1.1.1 Creation of a single regulator

After a period of '**self-regulation within a statutory framework**', 2001 saw a radical reform of the financial services system with the unification of most aspects of financial services regulation under a **single statutory regulator**, the **Financial Services Authority (FSA)**. The earlier 'patchwork quilt' of regulation was swept away and the FSA would regulate investment business, insurance business, banking, building societies, Friendly Societies, mortgages and Lloyd's.

New legislation came into force – the **Financial Services and Markets Act 2000** (FSMA 2000, often referred to just as FSMA) – creating a system of **statutory regulation**. While practitioners and consumers were actively consulted, it was the FSA that co-ordinated the regulation of the industry.

1.1.2 Responding to regulatory failures

The FSA regime sought to learn from many of the **regulatory failures** that occurred during the 1980s and 1990s, including a widespread problem of pensions mis-selling, the fraudulent collapse of the Bank of Credit and Commerce International, and the collapse of Barings Bank caused by a single rogue trader.

The regulation of the UK financial services industry has continued to evolve and to react to new circumstances as they develop. The financial crisis of the late 2000s stemmed in large part from excessive lending by banks, particularly to sub-prime borrowers, and from the 'securitisation' or packaging of mortgages by lenders for selling on to investors who were insufficiently aware of the risks attached to the securities. This period of turmoil has highlighted the need for continuing review and reform of regulatory arrangements.

1.1.3 Retail Distribution Review (RDR)

In addition to the 2013 regulatory re-structuring, another major recent change in the retail financial services sector is the implementation of the **Retail Distribution Review (RDR)**. The RDR seeks to make a clear distinction between **advice** and **sales** in the retail financial sector. The RDR changes took effect from **31 December 2012**.

Under the RDR rules, firms that give investment advice to retail clients must set their own charges, in agreement with their clients, and must meet new standards regarding how they determine and operate these charges. The changes have brought to an end the previous commission-based system of adviser remuneration: product providers are banned from offering amounts of commission to secure sales from adviser firms. Consumers are still able to have their adviser charges deducted from their investments if they wish, but these charges will no longer be determined by the product providers they are recommended.

1.2 Changing focus in the regulatory approach

After the establishment of the FSA, there were concerns about the extensive nature of regulation, and the volume of regulatory material which firms were having to follow. A 'twin approach' to supervising firms was heralded by the FSA, combining 'risk-based' and 'principles-based' aspects.

- The FSA's **risk-based approach** means that it focuses attention on those institutions and activities that are likely to pose the greatest risk to consumers and markets. The regulators consider it both impossible and undesirable to remove all risk from the financial system.

- The **principles-based** approach implies that, rather than formulate detailed rules to cover the varied circumstances firms are involved in, the Authority expect firms to carry more responsibility in making their own judgement about how to apply the regulatory Principles and Statements of Principle to their business. The regulator's initiative on **Treating Customers Fairly (TCF)** is an example of the its emphasis on principles.

In 2006, the FSA signalled its intention to shift, through time, towards greater reliance on **higher-level principles**, with fewer detailed rules and thus, potentially, a slimmer Handbook in future. There was some progress towards reduction in the volume of detailed rules.

The impact of principles-based regulation was also seen in **enforcement cases**, where the regulator invoked an expectation that firms would follow higher-level principles, even where there might not have been breaches of detailed rules.

Clearly, **front-line business personnel** should not, in general, be left to interpret higher level regulatory principles in how they carry out their work. The ongoing switch to a principles-based approach means that firms need to develop more of their own **internal rules**. **Senior management** will need to be involved in some of the more important rule-making decisions, which will not generally be left solely to the **compliance function**.

However, writing in the Chief Executive's Overview to the FSA's 2009/10 Business Plan, following the financial crisis, Hector Sants complained that the regulatory philosophy of **more principles-based regulation** had often been misunderstood. The focus of the Authority's philosophy, he wrote, is not *per se* on our principles, but rather on judging the consequences of the actions of the firms and the individuals we supervise. Given this philosophy, Sants argued, a better 'strapline' would be **outcomes-focused regulation**.

An example of this developing emphasis on **outcomes** is found in the regulator's approach to the principle of **treating customers fairly (TCF)**: as we shall see, the regulator has identified a number of TCF **consumer outcomes** against which firms are expected to measure their progress in meeting the TCF principle.

In practice, the regulator has aimed to strike a balance between principles and rules, with various corrective mechanisms being adopted to try to prevent any problems creating unacceptable levels of difficulty. The approach has also been referred to as being outcomes-, ownership-, accountability-, senior management-, anti-legalistic- and anti-bureaucratic-based regulation.

In the future, the regulators' supervisors are expected to evaluate the judgements of senior management and take appropriate measures if, in their view, those actions lead to risks to the regulatory objectives. This focus was seen by the FSA as a fundamental change, essentially ending '**reactive regulation**' based on facts and replacing it with regulation based on judgements about the future.

1: THE REGULATORY ENVIRONMENT

1.3 Re-structuring the regulatory framework

1.3.1 Overview

In mid-2010, with a Conservative-Liberal Democrat coalition Government in power, it was announced that the Financial Services Authority in its existing form would be abolished. The idea of abolishing the FSA and re-transferring core regulatory functions to the Bank of England was referred to by the Chancellor of the Exchequer in his 2010 Mansion House address.

- Under the reforms, there would be a sweeping increase in the powers of the **Bank of England**, which will have a new remit of preventing a build-up of risk in the financial system. At the top of the regulatory structure, a new subsidiary of the Bank based on the FSA's **Prudential Business Unit** (which was formed in April 2011), the **Prudential Regulation Authority (PRA)** is the **prudential regulator**, responsible for ensuring the safe operation of over 1,000 deposit-taking institutions, as well as insurers, investment banks and some other institutions.

- On 1 April 2013, the FSA legal entity became the **Financial Conduct Authority (FCA)**, which is responsible for consumer protection in financial services, the regulation of conduct of business (including in firms regulated by the new PRA) and market conduct. The **European Supervisory Authorities (ESAs)** will have the task of drawing up European standards including rules for consumer protection and financial innovation. The FCA will be the lead UK authority, active with the various ESAs in consumer protection activity.

> The **ESAs** cover banking, insurance and securities markets, and are: the European Banking Authority (EBA), the European Securities and Markets Authority (ESMA) and the European Insurance and Occupational Pensions Authority (EIOPA). Another key institution at the European level is the European Systemic Risk Board (ESRB), which has powers to issue warnings and recommendations on threats to economies and financial systems. **The syllabus does not require you to have knowledge of these institutions.**

1.3.2 'Blueprint for reform' (June 2011)

In 2011, the Government published a draft Bill and **White Paper** *A new approach to financial regulation: the blueprint for reform.*

Blueprint For Reform: key points

- Significant new powers were to be granted to the **Bank of England** with accountability being considered in parallel by the Treasury Select Committee. The BoE would be responsible for identifying potential crises and developing and implementing contingency plans. The Bank is made **responsible for ensuring the stability of the financial system**, and will be empowered to lead the response in a financial crisis. It is also proposed that responsibility for regulating settlement systems and recognised clearing houses (RCHs) is transferred to the BoE.

- The new **Financial Policy Committee (FPC)** would be set up **within the Bank of England**, with responsibility for macro-prudential oversight of the regulatory system. (**Macro-prudential policy** is concerned with monitoring risks and exposures across the financial system as a whole and not simply within one or more specific regulated sectors.)

- The **PRA** is being established as a **subsidiary of the Bank of England** to provide prudential regulation of firms which manage significant balance sheet risk as a core part of their business. This will include banks, insurers and the more complex investment firms. The PRA will have the power to designate firms that should fall within their scope, subject to certain procedural safeguards. (Prudential aspects of the operations of Lloyd's insurance market will be within the scope of the PRA.)

- The **FCA** will specialise in protecting customers and promoting confidence in financial services and markets, and promoting competition. The listing function (hitherto performed by the FSA) will be conferred on the FCA, which will thus act as the **UK Listing Authority (UKLA)**.

- The Blueprint emphasises the need for **coordination between the regulatory bodies**, as well as extensive **coordination with other bodies**, such as the **Financial Ombudsman Service (FOS)** and the Bank of England. The FPC has more flexibility regarding appointments of committee members to allow for swift changes in membership. The Government proposes to renew the FPC's remit annually. In an effort to make its workings transparent and accountable, records of FPC meetings will be published. It is envisaged that the FPC will publish two **Financial Stability Reports (FSRs)** a year, including a summary of its activities and an assessment of the effectiveness of its actions in the period since the last report. (The FPC will be able to exclude confidential or market-sensitive information from what it publishes.)

- The FOS is one of a **range of organisations** that will have the power to raise with the FCA **matters causing significant detriment** and the FCA will be required to consider appropriate action, which may include consumer redress.

1.3.3 Implementation of the reforms

The FSA had already moved to a **'twin peaks' operating model** in April 2012. This model largely reflects the way the two new organisations will operate in the future. The formal **re-structuring of the regulator into the PRA and FCA** – the so-called **'twin peaks' regulatory structure** – took place on **1 April 2013**. This date, when the PRA and FCA officially came into existence, is known as **'legal cutover' (LCO)**.

The Government is implementing the changes through amendment of FSMA 2000, rather than repeal of that Act. The **Financial Services Act 2012 (FSA 2012)** – the primary legislation that will bring the reforms into effect – came into force on the LCO date of 1 April 2013.

1.4 HM Treasury and the FCA

The minister with overall responsibility for the Treasury, the Chancellor of the Exchequer, is ultimately responsible for the regulatory system for financial services under FSMA 2000.

HM Treasury, to which the **FCA is accountable**, will judge the regulator against the requirements laid down in FSMA 2000 which includes a requirement to ensure that the burdens imposed on the regulated community are proportionate to the benefits it will provide.

Accountability of the FCA to HM Treasury

- HM Treasury has the power to **appoint or to dismiss the Board and Chairman of the FCA**.

- HM Treasury requires that the FCA submit an **annual report** covering such matters as the discharge of its functions and the extent to which the regulatory objectives have been met.

- HM Treasury also has powers to commission and publish an independent review of the **economy, efficiency and effectiveness** of the FCA's use of resources and to commission official enquiries into serious regulatory failures.

1: THE REGULATORY ENVIRONMENT

New UK regulatory architecture

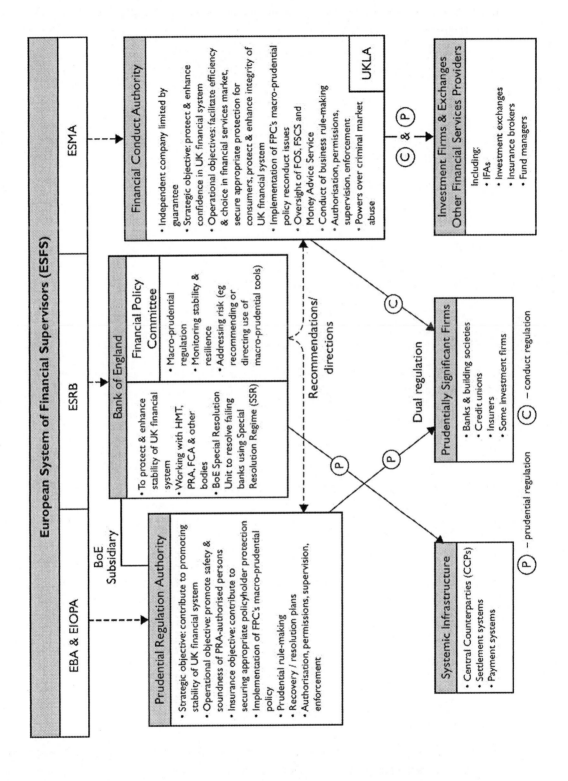

1: THE REGULATORY ENVIRONMENT

1.5 Prudential Regulation Authority (PRA)

The PRA is responsible for the prudential regulation of banks, insurance companies and large investment firms. Only these firms will be subject to '**dual regulation**' (see the diagram *New UK regulatory architecture*).

Under s2B FSMA 2000 (as amended by FSA 2012), the PRA is given a statutory **general objective** that is fundamentally different from that of earlier regulatory regimes:

Promoting the safety and soundness of PRA-authorised firms

The new Authority will meet this objective primarily by seeking to minimise any adverse effects of firm failure on the UK financial system and by ensuring that firms carry on their business in a way that avoids adverse effects on the system (s2B FSMA 2000).

Regarding insurance, the PRA has a more specific **insurance objective** of: contributing to the securing of an appropriate degree of protection for those who are or may become policyholders (s2C FSMA 2000).

The PRA will focus on the stability of the system overall, albeit through the mechanism of the supervision of individual firms. This will require close coordination with the new **Financial Policy Committee (FPC)** (see below), whose role it will be to manage the risks in the system as a whole. The PRA will be a key contributor to the information and analysis on which the FPC will base its judgements.

The PRA's supervisory efforts relating to financial stability will focus particularly on **large international banks**. In the case of UK subsidiaries of overseas banks, links of the UK entity with the group as a whole as well as the group's viability need to be an integral part of the PRA's supervisory assessment.

In order to deliver its objective of stability of the financial system, the PRA will use a new framework to assess risks to financial stability.

Key elements of PRA risk assessment framework

- Potential impact on the financial system of a firm coming under stress or failing
- Impact on the viability of a firm's business model of the macroeconomic and business risk context
- A firm's overall safety and soundness, which may act to mitigate the potential risk a firm poses to financial stability

Key mitigants to be assessed by the PRA

- Degree of resolvability of a firm (working closely with the Bank's Special Resolution Unit)
- The firm's financial strength (including its ability to generate capital through earnings, its capital held against future risks, the quality of its liquid assets and its liquidity management)
- The quality of a firm's risk management and governance (including the competence of its senior management)

Risks to a firm will be identified using:

- Baseline monitoring
- Investigation and assurance
- The macroeconomic and business context

The PRA will take a forward-looking and **judgment-based approach to supervision**. Baseline monitoring will be undertaken for all firms, including those that can be resolved with minimal disruption to the financial system (eg credit unions and small deposit-takers). This monitoring will include a review of a firm's resolvability (at least) once a year, analysis of a firm's financial position, discussions with senior management and ensuring compliance with minimum prudential standards for capital, liquidity and large exposures, as well as early interventions (where necessary) driven by a new **Proactive Intervention Framework (PIF)**, which we explain further in the next Chapter of this Study Text.

1.6 Bank of England

1.6.1 Core purposes

The Bank of England ('the Bank') – the central bank of the United Kingdom – plays an important role in the regulatory system. The Bank has two core purposes: to **ensure monetary stability** and to **contribute to financial stability**.

- **Monetary stability** means stable prices and confidence in the currency. Stable prices are defined by the Government's inflation target, which the Bank seeks to meet through the decisions delegated to the Monetary Policy Committee (which sets benchmark interest rates), explaining those decisions transparently and implementing them effectively in the money markets.

- **Financial stability** entails detecting and reducing threats to the financial system as a whole. This is pursued through the Bank's financial and other operations, including lender of last resort, oversight of key infrastructure and the surveillance and policy roles delegated to the Financial Policy Committee (FPC).

The Bank's **FPC** plays a key regulatory role, and the **PRA** is a subsidiary of the Bank.

1.6.2 Systemic financial crisis management

The Bank of England will have primary operational responsibility for **financial crisis management**.

When it is clear that **public funds may be put at risk**, the Governor of the BoE will have a statutory duty to notify the Chancellor.

A crisis management **memorandum of understanding (MoU)** underpins the process.

The MoU addresses:

- The responsibilities of the Bank and HM Treasury in a crisis
- The duty of the BoE to notify the Treasury of a risk to public funds
- The Chancellor's exercise of a power of direction over the Bank in a crisis

This process will now be backed up by a **statutory duty** to coordinate the exercise of these functions in a crisis.

As a power of last resort, the **Treasury** can direct the Bank:

- To provide liquidity support during a crisis, and
- To exercise its powers under the special resolution regime

The January 2012 New Approach paper (mentioned above) stresses that this power is exercisable only where there is a real risk to financial stability, or public funds have already been used, and that the BoE retains operational autonomy when managing threats to stability in which public funds are not at risk.

1.6.3 Financial Policy Committee (FPC)

The creation of the **Financial Policy Committee** was motivated by the perception that the absence of any effective macro-prudential agency was a major failing in the UK, EU and US before the recent financial crisis. This lack was highlighted with the inability of the authorities to deal with asset price bubbles, especially in the property market, and the accumulation of debt and leverage across the financial system.

The would-be functions of the Council for Financial Stability and the Bank of England's Financial Stability Committee have been merged into the FPC of the Bank. The FPC includes the FCA Chief Executive and representatives from HM Treasury. The FPC will also have some external representation and will meet four times annually and at times of crisis.

1: THE REGULATORY ENVIRONMENT

S9C Bank of England (BoE) Act 1998 (as amended by FSA 2012) provides that the FPC is to exercise its functions with a view to:

- Contributing to the achievement by the Bank of England of the **Financial Stability Objective**, and
- Subject to that, supporting the economic policy of the Government, including its objectives for growth and employment

The Bank's **Financial Stability Objective** is stated in s2A Bank of England Act 1998 (as amended by FSA 2012), which states that an objective of the Bank shall be: **To protect and enhance the stability of the financial system of the UK**.

The responsibility of the Committee in relation to the achievement by the Bank of the Financial Stability Objective relates primarily to the identification of, monitoring of, and taking of action to remove or reduce, **systemic risks** with a view to protecting and enhancing the resilience of the UK financial system (s9C(2) BoE Act 1998).

Those systemic risks include, in particular:

- Systemic risks attributable to structural features of financial markets, such as connections between financial institutions
- Systemic risks attributable to the distribution of risk within the financial sector, and
- Unsustainable levels of leverage, debt or credit growth (s9C(3) BoE Act 1998)

The legislation does not require or authorise the FPC to exercise its functions in a way that would in its opinion be likely to have a significant adverse effect on the capacity of the financial sector to contribute to the growth of the UK economy in the medium or long term.

Systemic risk here means a risk to the stability of the UK financial system as a whole or of a significant part of that system, whether the risk arises in the UK or elsewhere.

The **FPC** will have the following **tools** at its disposal:

- Setting system-wide cyclical capital requirements, reducing capital buffers required in a crisis while toughening them in more favourable economic times
- Altering risk weights, enabling the Bank to force banks to hold more capital against specific classes of assets in apparently frothy markets
- Setting limits on leverage as a backstop against excessive lending where changing risk weights might not be effective
- Requiring forward-looking loss provisioning to prepare for future losses when lending growth is strong
- Setting limits on borrowing, eg with maximum loan-to-value ratios for mortgages
- Setting limits on lending through regulation

The Treasury has indicated that the **Chancellor of the Exchequer** would however retain the right to **overrule the Bank of England Governor** in a crisis.

1.7 Financial Conduct Authority (FCA)

1.7.1 Strategic objective

The FSA 2012 gives the new **Financial Conduct Authority (FCA)** a single **strategic objective**:

'Ensuring that the relevant markets function well' (s1B(2) FSMA 2000, as amended by FSA 2012)

1.7.2 Operational objectives

This strategic objective will be supported by three **operational objectives**:

- **The consumer protection objective**: securing an appropriate degree of protection for consumers
- **The integrity objective:** protecting and enhancing the integrity of the UK financial system
- **The competition objective**: promoting effective competition in the interests of consumers in the market for regulated financial services and for services provided by a recognised investment exchange

The Authority will also have duties to **promote competition** (which may involve analysing pricing) and to **address financial crime** (broadly, following the existing approach to tackling such crime).

In an October 2012 speech, a spokesperson for the regulator explained that the FCA was being set up to work with firms with the aim of ensuring that they put **consumers at the heart of their business**. Underlining this are three **outcomes**:

- Consumers get financial services and products that meet their needs from firms they can trust
- Firms compete effectively with the interests of their customers and the integrity of the market at the heart of how they run their business
- Markets and financial systems are sound, stable and resilient with transparent pricing information

1.7.3 Consumer protection objective

In considering what degree of **protection for consumers** may be appropriate, the FCA must have regard to (s1C FSMA 2000):

- The differing degrees of risk involved in different kinds of investment or other transaction
- The differing degrees of experience and expertise that different consumers may have
- The needs that consumers may have for the timely provision of information and advice that is accurate and fit for purpose
- The general principle that consumers should take responsibility for their decisions
- The general principle that those providing regulated financial services should be expected to provide consumers with a level of care that is appropriate having regard to the degree of risk involved in relation to the investment or other transaction and the capabilities of the consumers in question
- The differing expectations that consumers may have in relation to different kinds of investment or other transaction
- Any information which the consumer financial education body has provided to the FCA in the exercise of the consumer financial education function
- Any information which the scheme operator of the ombudsman scheme has provided to the FCA

1.7.4 Integrity objective

Regarding this objective, the **integrity of the UK financial system** includes (s1D FSMA 2000):

- Its soundness, stability and resilience
- Its not being used for a purpose connected with financial crime
- Its not being affected by behaviour that amounts to market abuse
- The orderly operation of the financial markets, and
- The transparency of the price formation process in those markets

1.7.5 Competition objective

The matters to which the FCA may have regard in considering the **effectiveness of competition** include:

- The needs of different consumers who use or may use those services, including their need for information that enables them to make informed choices
- The ease with which consumers who may wish to use those services, including consumers in areas affected by social or economic deprivation, can access them
- The ease with which consumers who obtain those services can change the person from whom they obtain them
- The ease with which new entrants can enter the market, and
- How far competition is encouraging innovation

1.7.6 Aspects of the FCA's functions

The FCA will not of course be starting from scratch, but the FCA will be more interventionist than the FSA was. It will build upon existing initiatives such as the FSA's **Consumer Protection Strategy**.

Smaller investment firms will continue to be supervised by a **single regulator** under the new regulatory structure, but this will be the **FCA**, rather than the FSA as in the past. Thus, the FCA will be responsible for both prudential and conduct regulation for these firms, as illustrated in the earlier diagram showing the *New UK regulatory architecture*.

It is proposed that the FCA's **supervisory model** will have the following elements.

- A revised **risk assessment process** (replacing the FSA's 'ARROW' framework) that can be communicated to senior executives and boards of firms, thus enabling good business practice to be aligned with good regulatory practice (we will outline the FCA's risk assessment process in more detail in Chapter 2 of this Study Text)
- In response to the regulatory problems that have arisen since 1990, a **lower risk tolerance** than under the previous regulatory regime: this may mean (using new powers under FSMA 2000, as amended by FSA 2012) banning products before they reach the market, or banning a firm from selling a widely accepted product if its sales processes are unacceptable

As an 'integrated conduct' regulator, the FCA will look across the whole financial services sector, not only in **investment and capital markets** but also in **banking and wholesale insurance markets**. Under its consumer protection remit, the Authority will define 'consumer' as including even the largest wholesale firms. This will enable the FCA to exercise wide discretion over the interpretation of its objectives and to ensure high standards across the financial services industry in the service of its strategic objective.

The new Authority will set out to recognise that wholesale activities can have a direct impact on retail markets. It will need to consider the interactions and linkages across the financial value chain where risks are transmitted between wholesale and retail customers. In particular, the FCA will look at intervention further up the value chain, targeted at **product governance**. Where activity in wholesale markets may lead to mis-conceived, overly complicated or confusing products, aimed at the mass market, the FCA would plan to intervene.

Clearly the intention of the senior management that is planned to run the new Authority is to develop a new culture, given the perceived regulatory failures of recent years. Speech-making to launch the FCA has spoken of a **pro-active 'can do' approach**, and of the new Authority being **bold** in the use of its powers.

1.8 FCA and PRA supervision

Firms that are '**dual regulated**' – by both the FCA and the PRA – such as banks, insurers and major investment firms, will be supervised by two independent groups within the regulators for **prudential** and **conduct**. These groups will work to different objectives and act separately with firms, but will coordinate internally to share information and data.

All other firms will be supervised by one supervision area for both conduct and prudential issues.

The supervision models will be different for the PRA and FCA:

- Prudential supervision will continue to have dedicated resources supervising firms, and
- Conduct supervision will focus more on thematic work, and less on firm-specific work

1.9 Powers of the regulators

The **powers** of the new regulators – the FCA and the PRA – include the following. (Note that the term '**firm**' is used generally in the regulations to apply to an authorised person, whether the person is an individual, a partnership or a corporate body.)

- Granting **authorisation** and **permission** to firms (under **Part 4A** of FSMA 2000) to undertake regulated activities
- **Approving** individuals to perform controlled functions
- Issuing (under **Part 9A FSMA 2000**):
    - (In the case of the FCA) general **rules** for authorised firms which appear to be necessary or expedient to advance the FCA's operational objectives (such as the **Conduct of Business** rules, and rules on firms holding clients' money)
    - (In the case of the PRA) general **rules** for PRA-authorised firms which appear to be necessary or expedient to advance the PRA's objectives
- **Supervision** of authorised firm to ensure that they continue to meet the regulators' authorisation requirements and that they comply with the regulatory rules and other obligations
- Powers to take **enforcement** action against authorised firms and approved persons
- Powers to **discipline** authorised firms and approved persons

The **FCA** has powers to:

- Take action against any person for **insider dealing** or **market abuse**
- **Recognise** investment exchanges and clearing houses
- As the **UK Listing Authority**, approve companies for stock exchange listings in the UK

The FCA oversees the **Financial Ombudsman Service (FOS)** and the **Money Advice Service**.

The FCA and PRA jointly oversee the **Financial Services Compensation Scheme (FSCS)**.

1.10 Evaluating the re-structuring plans

Arguments raised about the re-structuring proposals have concerned breaking-up an apparently less effective monolithic authority (while at the same as creating an even larger one), separating prudential from consumer protection and market oversight, promoting the Bank's expertise in economic monitoring and integrating market oversight with market support (traditionally referred to as the role of lender of last resort).

1: THE REGULATORY ENVIRONMENT

- **Advantages** of the new regime include more focused and dedicated supervision, tailored regulation, separate agency mandates, additional powers and possible prioritisation of action and function.

- **Disadvantages** include the inconsistent treatment of consumer protection and market oversight, the potentially systemic effect of market failure, the need to promote consumer and market confidence, the split enforcement function, the institutional separation arising from creating the PRA as a subsidiary rather than division of the Bank, possible over-centralisation of the macro-prudential function and decision-taking, linkage created between monetary and financial stability policy, substantial cost and significant regulatory obligations imposed and consequent market and competitive disruption created.

The most important justification for the new regime is the establishment of a strong **macro-prudential function** within the UK regulatory system. While this will be carried out by the FPC, this was previously dealt with by the internal Financial Stability Committee (FSC) set up within the Bank of England under the Banking Act 2009 and the external Council for Financial Stability (CFS) which replaced the earlier Tripartite Committee.

While the need for a strong macro-prudential function is generally accepted, it is less clear whether a separate twin peaks division of prudential and conduct regulation was necessary or whether this could have been more effectively dealt with within a larger, better funded FSA divided into two separate prudential and conduct divisions. This could arguably more clearly reflect the integrated and interconnected nature of modern financial markets.

2 PRINCIPLES FOR BUSINESSES

> **Learning Objective**: Understand the Principles for Businesses and the requirement to act honestly, fairly and professionally and to treat customers fairly

2.1 Introduction

The **Principles for Businesses** state firms' fundamental obligations under the regulatory system. They are formulated to require honest, fair and professional conduct from firms.

The **Principles for Businesses** are included in both the **PRA and FCA** Handbooks. They are referred to as **PRIN** in the Handbooks.

2.2 Application of the Principles

PRIN applies in whole or in part to every **authorised firm** carrying out a regulated activity. (They are distinct from the **Statements of Principle for Approved Persons**, which cover individuals rather than firms and which we shall look at later.)

2.3 The Principles for Businesses

The eleven **Principles for Businesses** are as follows.

Principles for Businesses
1. Integrity   A firm must conduct its business with integrity.
2. Skill, care and diligence   A firm must conduct its business with due skill, care and diligence.
3. Management and control   A firm must take reasonable care to organise and control its affairs responsibly and effectively, with adequate risk management systems.
4. Financial prudence   A firm must maintain adequate financial resources.
5. Market conduct   A firm must observe proper standards of market conduct.
6. Customers' interests   A firm must pay due regard to the interests of its customers and treat them fairly.
7. Communications with clients   A firm must pay due regard to the information needs of its clients and communicate information to them in a way that is clear, fair and not misleading.
8. Conflicts of interest   A firm must manage conflicts of interest fairly, both between itself and its customers and between a customer and another client.
9. Customers: relationships of trust   A firm must take reasonable care to ensure the suitability of its advice and discretionary decisions for any customer who is entitled to rely upon its judgement.
10. Clients' assets   A firm must arrange adequate protection for clients' assets when it is responsible for those assets.
11. Relations with regulators   A firm must deal with its regulators in an open and co-operative way and must disclose to the appropriate regulator appropriately anything relating to the firm of which that regulator would reasonably expect notice.

2.4 Scope of the Principles

Some of the principles (such as Principle 10) refer to **clients**, while others (such as Principle 9) refer to **customers**. This difference affects the scope of the relevant Principles.

- '**Client**' is an all-encompassing term that includes everyone from the smallest retail customer through to the largest investment firm. It therefore includes, under the terminology of MiFID, eligible counterparties, professional customers and retail customers.

- '**Customer**' is a more restricted term that includes professional and retail clients but excludes 'eligible counterparties''. 'Customers' are thus clients who are not **eligible counterparties**. (We shall see later what is meant by this term.) Principles 6, 8 and 9, and parts of Principle 7, apply only to **customers**.

In line with MiFID, a firm will not be subject to a Principle to the extent that it is contrary to the EU Single Market Directives. Principles 1, 2, 6 and 9 may be disapplied for this reason, in the case of:

- Eligible counterparty business
- Transactions on a regulated market (eg the London Stock Exchange), and member transactions under a **multilateral trading facility (MTF)** – a system that enables parties (eg retail investors or other investment firms) to buy and sell financial instruments

Note that Principle 3 would not be considered breached if the firm failed to prevent **unforeseeable** risks.

2.5 Breaches of the Principles

The consequence of breaching a Principle is that the firm becomes liable to **enforcement or disciplinary sanctions**. The regulators may bring these sanctions where it can show that the firm has been at fault in some way. The definition of 'fault' will depend which Principle has potentially been breached.

Section 150 FSMA 2000 creates a right of action in damages for a '**private person**' who suffers loss as a result of a contravention of certain **rules** by an authorised firm. However, a 'private person' may not sue a firm under s150 FSMA 2000 for the breach of a **Principle**.

2.6 Treating customers fairly (TCF)

In addition to meeting its regulatory objectives, as previous regulator the FSA aimed to maintain efficient, orderly and clean markets and help retail customers achieve a fair deal. The regulator examined what a fair deal for retail customers actually means and this led to much discussion of the concept of **TCF – 'treating customers fairly'**. This work, started by the FSA, will be continued by the FCA.

Principle for Businesses 6 states that a firm must pay due regard to its customers and treat them fairly. By adopting a 'principles-based approach' to TCF through Principle 6, the regulator places the onus on firms to determine what is fair in each particular set of circumstances. Firms therefore need to make their own assessment of what TCF means for them, taking into account the nature of their business.

The emphasis of the regulator's philosophy is not so much on the principles themselves. It is on the actual consequences of what firms do. Increasingly, as we saw earlier, the term used for the more recent approach (in 2009 and beyond) has been **outcomes-focused regulation**.

TCF has been treated as a part of the **regulator's core supervisory work**. Firms – meaning senior management, including the Board – are expected to be able to demonstrate to themselves and to the regulator that they deliver **fair outcomes to their customers**.

With regard to TCF, the regulator specifically wants firms to focus on delivering the following six **consumer outcomes**.

- Consumers can be confident that they are dealing with firms where the fair treatment of customers is central to the corporate culture.
- Products and services marketed and sold in the retail market are designed to meet the needs of identified consumer groups and are targeted accordingly.
- Consumers are provided with clear information and are kept appropriately informed before, during, and after the point of sale.
- Where consumers receive advice, the advice is suitable and takes account of their circumstances.

- Consumers are provided with products that perform as firms have led them to expect, and the associated service is both of an acceptable standard and also as they have been led to expect.
- Consumers do not face unreasonable post-sale barriers imposed by firms to change product, switch provider, submit a claim or make a complaint.

2.7 The client's best interests rule

The **Conduct of Business Rules** require that:

- Firms must act honestly, fairly and professionally in accordance with the **best interests of the client**.

This is the **client's best interests rule**.

This important rule applies to designated investment business for a retail client or, in relation to MiFID business, for any other client. ('Designated investment business' includes various regulated activities but not deposits, mortgages nor non-savings insurance contracts.)

In communications relating to designated investment business, a firm must not seek to **exclude or restrict any duty or liability** it may have under the **regulatory system**. If the client is a retail client, any other exclusion or restriction of duties or liabilities must meet the 'clients' best interests rule' test above. (The general law, including **unfair terms regulations**, also limits a firm's scope for excluding or restricting duties or liabilities to a consumer.)

3 STATEMENTS OF PRINCIPLE FOR APPROVED PERSONS

> **Learning Objectives**
>
> **Know** the Statements of Principle 1 to 4 and Code of Practice for approved persons for all approved person functions
>
> **Know** the Statements of Principle 5 to 7 and Code of Practice for approved persons in respect of significant influence functions

3.1 Approved persons

Section 59 FSMA 2000 states that a person (an individual) cannot carry out certain **controlled functions** unless that individual has been approved by the relevant regulator. This requirement gives rise to the term '**approved person**', and the Supervision Manual (SUP) covers the approval process. We look further at the approval process, and at what are controlled functions, in Chapter 2 of this Study Text.

3.2 The Statements of Principle

The **Statements of Principle** apply generally to all **approved persons** (ie relevant employees of regulated firms) when they are performing a **controlled function**. The scope of 'controlled' functions is covered in Chapter 2 of this Study Text.

The Statements of Principle will not apply where it would be contrary to the UK's obligations under EU Single Market Directives. Under **MiFID** rules, the requirement to employ personnel with the necessary knowledge, skills and expertise is reserved to the firm's **Home State**. As a result, the regulator does not have a role in assessing individuals' competence and capability in performing a controlled function in relation to an **incoming EEA firm** providing MiFID investment services.

There are **seven Statements of Principle**. The first four Principles apply to all approved persons (which includes those performing a **significant influence function** as well as those not doing a significant influence function).

As shown in the following Table, the final three Principles apply only to approved persons performing a significant influence function. The **PRA** will have primary responsibility for the designation and regulation of **significant influence** functions.

Statements of Principle for Approved Persons	
1 Integrity	Apply to all approved persons
2 Skill, care and diligence	
3 Proper standard of market conduct	
4 Deal with the regulators in an open way	
5 Proper organisation of business	Apply only to those performing a significant influence function
6 Skill, care and diligence in management	
7 Comply with regulatory requirements	

3.3 The Code of Practice for Approved Persons

FSMA 2000 requires the regulator to issue a code of practice to help approved persons to determine whether or not their conduct complies with the Statements of Principle. This is entitled the **Code of Practice for Approved Persons**. This sets out descriptions of conduct which, in the regulator's opinion, does not comply with any of the statements, and factors which will be taken into account in determining whether or not an approved person's conduct does comply with the Statements of Principle. These descriptions have the status of **evidential provisions**.

The Code is not conclusive – it is only evidential towards indicating that a Statement of Principle has been breached. Account will be taken of the context in which the course of conduct was undertaken. In determining whether there has been a breach of Principles 5 to 7, account will be taken of the nature and complexity of the business, the role and responsibilities of the approved person, and the knowledge that the approved person had (or should have had) of the regulatory concerns arising in the business under their control. The examples in the Code that would breach a principle are not exhaustive.

The Code may be amended from time to time and the current published version at the time of the approved person's conduct will be the Code that the regulator will look to in determining whether or not there has been a breach. The regulator will examine all the circumstances of a particular matter and will only determine that there has been a breach where the individual is **'personally culpable'**, ie deliberate conduct or conduct below the reasonable standard expected of that person in the circumstances.

We now look at the **seven Statements of Principle** in detail, taking into account the treatment of each by the **Code of Practice for Approved Persons**.

3.4 The Statements of Principle in detail

Statement of Principle 1

An approved person must act with integrity in carrying out his controlled function.

The Code of Practice provides examples of behaviour that would not comply with this Statement of Principle. These include an approved person:

- **Deliberately misleading clients**, his firm or the regulator, or
- Deliberately failing to inform a customer, his firm, or the regulator, that their understanding of a material issue is incorrect.

Statement of Principle 2

> An approved person must act with due skill, care and diligence in carrying out his controlled function.

Examples of non-compliant behaviour under Statement of Principle 2 include failing to inform a **customer**, or his firm, of material information or failing to control client assets.

The coverage of Statement of Principle 2 is similar to Principle 1. The difference is that Principle 1 states that each act needs to be **deliberate**. Principle 2 may be breached by acts which, while not deliberate wrongdoing, are **negligent**.

Statement of Principle 3

> An approved person must observe proper standards of market conduct in carrying out his controlled function.

Examples of non-compliant behaviour under Statement of Principle 3 include:

- A breach of market codes and exchange rules, or
- A breach of the *Code of Market Conduct*

The regulators expect all approved persons to meet proper standards, whether they are participating in organised markets such as exchanges, or trading in less formal over-the-counter markets.

Statement of Principle 4

> An approved person must deal with the regulators in an open and co-operative way and must disclose appropriately any information of which the regulators would reasonably expect notice.

This Statement of Principle concerns the requirement to co-operate, not only with the regulators, but also with other bodies such as an overseas regulator or an exchange.

Approved persons do not have a duty to report concerns directly to the regulator unless they are responsible for such reports. The obligation on most approved persons is to report concerns of '**material significance**' in accordance with the firm's **internal procedures**. If no such procedures exist, the report should be made direct to the regulator.

It would also be a breach of this Statement of Principle if an approved person did not attend an interview or meeting with the regulator, answer questions or produce documents when requested to do so, and within the time limit specified.

Statement of Principle 5

> An approved person performing a significant influence function must take reasonable steps to ensure that the business of the firm for which he is responsible in his controlled function is organised so that it can be controlled effectively.

As stated above, Principles 5 to 7 relate only to those approved persons performing a significant influence function. This principle requires those performing a significant influence function to **delegate** responsibilities responsibly and effectively. Paramount to this is a requirement that they should delegate only where it is to a suitable person. In addition, they must provide those persons with proper reporting lines, authorisation levels and job descriptions. Clearly, all of these factors (and in particular the suitability requirement) should be regularly reviewed.

Principle 5 will be particularly relevant to the person whose responsibility it is to ensure appropriate apportionment of responsibilities under the Senior Management Arrangements, Systems and Controls (**SYSC**) section which appears in both the FCA and PRA Handbooks.

Statement of Principle 6

> An approved person performing a significant influence function must exercise due skill, care and diligence in managing the business of the firm for which he is responsible in his controlled function.

This principle requires those performing a significant influence function to inform themselves about the affairs of the business for which they are responsible. They should not permit transactions or an expansion of the business unless they fully **understand the risks** involved. They must also take care when monitoring highly profitable or unusual transactions and in those or other cases, must never accept implausible or unsatisfactory explanations from subordinates.

This principle links to Principle 5 as it makes it clear that **delegation is not an abdication** of responsibility. Therefore, where delegation has been made, a person must still monitor and control that part of the business and, therefore, should require progress reports and question those reports where appropriate.

Statement of Principle 7

> An approved person performing a significant influence function must take reasonable steps to ensure that the business of the firm for which he is responsible in his controlled function complies with the relevant requirements and standards of the regulatory system.

This has a clear link to Principle 3 of the *Principles for Businesses – Management and Control.* Those exerting a significant influence on the firm must take reasonable steps to ensure that the requirements set out therein are implemented within their firm. They should also review the improvement of such systems and controls, especially where there has been a breach of the regulatory requirements. Principle 7 will be particularly relevant to the person whose responsibility it is to ensure appropriate apportionment of responsibilities under SYSC.

4 CISI's Code of Conduct

Learning Objective — **Know** the Chartered Institute for Securities and Investment's Code of Conduct

4.1 Overview

The **Chartered Institute for Securities & Investment (CISI)** is a widely respected professional body for those working in the securities and investment industry.

You should familiarise yourself with the CISI's Professional Code of Conduct.

4.2 Professional Code of Conduct

The Institute has stated that 'professionals within the securities and investment industry owe important **duties to their clients**, to the market, the industry and to society at large. Where these duties are set out in law or in regulation, the professional must always comply with the requirements in an open and transparent manner.'

Members of the Chartered Institute for Securities & Investment are **required** to meet the standards set out within the Institute's Principles. These principles, also known as the Lord George Principles, impose an obligation on members to act in a way beyond mere compliance and to support the underlying values of the Institute.

Material breach of the Code of Conduct would be incompatible with continuing membership of the CISI and may result in disciplinary action.

Members who find themselves in a position which might require them to act in a manner contrary to the Principles are encouraged to:

1. Discuss their concerns with their line manager
2. Seek advice from their internal compliance department
3. Approach their firm's non-executive directors or audit committee
4. If unable to resolve their concerns and, having exhausted all internal avenues, contact the CISI for advice (e-mail: principles@cisi.org)

Code of Conduct: Principles

1. To act honestly and fairly at all times when dealing with clients, customers and counterparties and to be a good steward of their interests, taking into account the nature of the business relationship with each of them, the nature of the service to be provided to them and the individual mandates given by them.
2. To act with integrity in fulfilling the responsibilities of your appointment and seek to avoid any acts, omissions or business practices which damage the reputation of your organisation or the financial services industry.
3. To observe applicable law, regulations and professional conduct standards when carrying out financial service activities, and to interpret and apply them to the best of your ability according to principles rooted in trust, honesty and integrity.
4. To observe the standards of market integrity, good practice and conduct required or expected of participants in markets when engaged in any form of market dealings.
5. To be alert to and manage fairly and effectively and to the best of your ability any relevant conflict of interest.
6. To attain and actively manage a level of professional competence appropriate to your responsibilities, to commit to continuing learning to ensure the currency of your knowledge, skills and expertise and to promote the development of others.
7. To decline to act in any matter about which you are not competent unless you have access to such advice and assistance as will enable you to carry out the work in a professional manner.
8. To strive to uphold the highest personal and professional standards.

1: THE REGULATORY ENVIRONMENT

5 SENIOR MANAGEMENT RESPONSIBILITIES

> **Learning Objective**: **Understand** the rules regarding Senior Management Arrangements, Systems and Controls for both common platform firms and non-MiFID firms

5.1 Overview

The regulator has drafted a large amount of guidance on **PRIN 3** (Principle for Businesses 3). You may recall that this Principle is as follows.

> **Management and control**: 'A firm must take reasonable care to organise and control its affairs responsibly and effectively, with adequate risk management systems.'

This regulatory emphasis on senior management responsibilities, which we mentioned earlier in this Chapter, came particularly from a desire to avoid a repetition of the collapse of Barings Bank, where it was clear that management methods and the control environment were deficient.

Note that it would not be a breach of this Principle if the firm failed to prevent **unforeseeable** risks.

The regulator suggests that, in order to comply with its obligation to maintain appropriate systems, a firm should carry out a regular review of the relevant factors.

As already mentioned, there is a section of the FCA and PRA Handbooks called '**Senior Management Arrangements, Systems and Controls**'. As the name suggests, the main purpose of this part of the Handbook is to encourage directors and senior managers of authorised firms to take appropriate responsibility for their firm's arrangements and to ensure they know what those obligations are.

> **Exam tip**: The examiner may refer to this Handbook section by its abbreviation **SYSC**.

5.2 SYSC requirements

A significant requirement of SYSC is the need for the Chief Executive to apportion duties amongst senior management and to monitor their performance. Beyond this, the main issues that a firm is expected to consider in establishing compliance with Principle 3 are as follows.

- Organisation and reporting lines
- Compliance
- Risk assessment
- Suitable employees and agents
- Audit committee
- Remuneration policies

There is a rule regarding **apportionment of significant responsibilities**, which requires firms to make clear who has particular responsibility and to ensure that the business of the firm can be adequately monitored and controlled by the directors, senior management and the firm's governing body. Details of apportionment and allocation of responsibilities must be recorded and kept up-to-date.

Under **SYSC**, the firm has a general obligation to take reasonable care to establish and maintain systems and controls that are appropriate to its business. MiFID firms are required to **monitor and regularly evaluate** the adequacy of its systems, internal control mechanisms and arrangements established to comply with the above. Firms are likely to have to keep additional documentation to fully meet this requirement.

Furthermore, the **compliance function** must be designed for the purpose of complying with regulatory requirements and to counter the risk that the firm may be used to further financial crime.

Sole traders without anyone performing **controlled functions** and therefore requiring to be an **approved person** are exempt from many of the SYSC requirements set out here (for example, the requirement to have a Money Laundering Reporting Officer (MLRO)).

SYSC sets out rules (in SYSC 4–10, as summarised below) that are known as the **common platform**.

- Although originally, non-MiFID firms were not required to follow the 'common platform' rules, the common platform was extended beyond MiFID firms with effect from 1 April 2009.
- Now, most firms come within the common platform, and the only firms outside it are insurers, managing agents and the Society of Lloyd's.

5.2.1 General requirements

Adequate policies and procedures rule. Taking into account the nature and complexity of its business, and the activities undertaken, a **common platform firm** must put in place policies and procedures designed to detect any risk of failure by the firm to meet its regulatory obligations and to minimise any associated risks. The procedures must enable regulatory authorities to exercise their powers effectively.

Compliance function rule. Common platform firms must maintain a permanent, independent and effective compliance function.

The **compliance function** must have:

- The necessary authority, expertise and access to relevant information
- A compliance officer, responsible for the function and for reporting
- Those involved in compliance not to be involved in performing services or activities they monitor, and to have remuneration which is not likely to compromise their objectivity (but firms need not comply with these two requirements if they can show that their compliance function continues to be effective)

Firms must have **robust governance arrangements**, which include a clear organisational structure with well-defined, transparent and consistent lines of responsibility; effective processes to identify, manage, monitor and report the risks it is or might be exposed to; and internal control mechanisms, including sound administrative and accounting procedures and effective control and safeguard arrangements for information processing systems. For common platform firms, the arrangements must be comprehensive and proportionate.

Reporting lines, functions and responsibilities must be specified and documented, and internal control mechanisms must be adequate. Firms' procedures must safeguard the security, integrity and confidentiality of information.

Systems, internal control mechanisms and arrangements must take into account the nature, scale and complexity of the business and the range of its activities. Common platform firms must monitor and evaluate them regularly, addressing any deficiencies.

Senior personnel and (where appropriate) the **supervisory function** are responsible for ensuring compliance with regulatory obligations and must, in common platform firms, receive frequent (at least annual) reports on remedial measures taken to address deficiencies.

Firms must employ **personnel with the skills, knowledge and expertise** necessary for the discharge of their responsibilities.

Common platform firms must have a separate and independent **internal audit function**, with responsibility for maintaining an **audit plan** to examine and evaluate the adequacy and effectiveness of systems and internal controls, and for issuing recommendations and verifying compliance with them.

Firms must ensure that its procedures allow it to identify, assess, monitor and manage **money laundering risk**.

A director or senior manager (who may be the MLRO) must have overall responsibility for a firm's anti-money laundering (AML) **systems and controls**.

Firms must appoint an **MLRO**, who has sufficient authority, independence and access to resources and information, with responsibility for overseeing the regulatory rules on anti-money laundering systems and controls.

There are requirements for common platform firms (and guidance for other firms) to:

- Establish, implement and maintain adequate **risk management policies** and procedures which identify and set the tolerable level of risk relating to a firm's activities including employees' compliance with them; and

- Have a separate **risk control function**, where this is proportionate, depending on the nature, scale and complexity of its business.

5.2.2 Outsourcing

The regulators believe that the **operational risk** posed by **outsourcing** arrangements presents a significant threat to the statutory objectives of securing the appropriate degree of protection for consumers, maintaining confidence in the financial system and of reducing financial crime. This is mainly because outsourcing arrangements have the potential to transfer risk, management and compliance to third parties who may not be regulated and may operate offshore.

The SYSC requirements for firms to have robust governance arrangements and adequate internal control mechanisms cover all outsourcing arrangements both material (critical or important) and non-material in relation to the firm's whole business. The regulators consider that non-material outsourcing is not entirely risk-free and therefore will give management the flexibility of applying controls to non-material outsourcing in a manner which is appropriate and proportionate to the firm's needs. The regulator is not going to give guidance on what is meant by 'material' because what is material is likely to vary according to the nature and circumstances of each firm.

Two conditions are applied where a MiFID investment firm outsources **portfolio management provided to retail clients** to a service provider located in a **non-EEA** (third) country.

The firm must ensure that:

- The service provider is authorised or registered in its home country to provide that service and is subject to prudential supervision, and

- There is an appropriate co-operation agreement between the regulator and the competent authority of the service provider

If one or both of the above conditions is not satisfied, the regulator must be informed and may raise an objection, within one month of being informed.

5.2.3 Record-keeping

Record keeping. Firms are required to arrange for orderly **records** to be kept of its business and internal organisation, including all services and transactions undertaken. The records must be sufficient to enable the regulator (or other competent authority) to:

- Monitor compliance with the requirements under the regulatory system
- Ascertain that the firm has complied with all obligations with respect to clients and potential clients

MiFID requires firms to keep transaction records for **five years**. For non-MiFID business, some other time limits apply to particular types of business.

5.3 Remuneration Code (SYSC 19A)

5.3.1 Overview

The first Remuneration Code was implemented at the beginning of 2010. In December 2010, the previous regulator (the FSA) published an updated **Remuneration Code**, implemented in early 2011, to take into account changes required by the revised **Capital Requirements Directive (CRD3)**. CRD3 aims to align remuneration principles across the EU.

Even so, investment banks have been reported (*Financial Times*, 21 October 2011) to have been exploiting **loopholes** in remuneration rules and persisting with contentious practices such as guaranteeing an element of staff bonuses regardless of performance. This practice is seen as jeopardising risk management by severing the link between performance and reward. Additionally, most leading banks have increased fixed salaries, compensating staff for the effect of the reforms that require a larger proportion of bonuses to be paid as shares and over a multi-year period.

As well as needing to follow regulatory provisions on remuneration, financial firms have become more mindful of growing shareholder activism over executive pay and bonuses.

The Code applies to a group of firms including all banks and building societies and CAD investment firms – some 2,700 in total.

A **proportionate** approach will be applied to implementation of the Code in line with the purpose of the previous Code to ensure remuneration policies promote effective risk management. The proportionate approach allows firms to comply 'in a way and to the extent that is appropriate to its size, internal organisation and the nature, the scope and the complexity of its activities'. Accordingly, there will be four tiers of firms with differing minimum expectations of compliance for each group:

5.3.2 Scope: staff covered

The Remuneration Code covers staff (called '**code staff**') whose professional activities have a material impact on the firm's risk profile and who fall into one of four categories:

- Senior management
- Risk takers
- Staff engaged in control functions, and
- Any employee whose remuneration is in the same bracket as senior management and risk-takers

5.3.3 Remuneration definition

The regulator defines **remuneration** as being any aspect of compensation that can have a bearing on effective risk management. This definition covers signing-on and severance packages, pensions, options and long-term incentive plans, as well as salaries and bonuses.

5.3.4 The Code

The revised (1 January 2011) Code is based on a set of **principles** that are underpinned by Principle 1.

Principle 1 requires firms to put in place a remuneration policy that:

- Is consistent with and promotes sound and effective risk management, and
- Does not encourage risk-taking that exceeds the level of tolerated risk of the firm

Other Principles in the Code include:

- Avoidance of conflicts of interest
- Ensuring that a firm's remuneration practices do not endanger its capital base

1: THE REGULATORY ENVIRONMENT

- Basing assessments of financial performance on profit, and
- Ensuring that employees undertake not to use personal hedging strategies to offset the risk-based approach to their compensation

Controversially, **Principle 12** sets out the following new requirements for remuneration structures, which must be adhered to subject to the principle of proportionality.

- Remuneration must be structured so as to promote effective risk management
- Performance-related remuneration must take into account individual, business unit and firm-wide performance and must encompass non-financial performance metrics
- Guarantees should be exceptional, for new hires only and limited to a year
- Firms must set appropriate ratios between fixed and variable elements of total compensation
- Early termination payments should not reward failure
- At least 50% of both the deferred and non-deferred elements of variable remuneration should consist of shares, ownership interests, share-linked instruments and/or equivalent non-cash instruments that are subject to a retention policy to align incentives with the firm's long-term interests
- At least 40% of variable remuneration should be deferred over a minimum period of 3 to 5 years and deferred remuneration must vest no faster than on a pro-rata basis
- For staff whose remuneration has a variable component of over £500,000, 60% should be deferred
- Variable remuneration should be paid or vest only if justified by the performance of the firm, business unit and employee; the firm should adjust unvested elements of remuneration if warranted by subsequent circumstances

It is perhaps still too early to assess whether the Remuneration Code has had any material impact on remuneration structures in the sector, or on the excessive risk-taking that the regulator intended to rein back. However, in the context of continuing 'austerity' measures affecting the wider population, remuneration in the financial sector may continue to be a contentious issue for the foreseeable future.

6 REGULATORY INFRASTRUCTURE

> **Learning Objective**
>
> **Know** the wider structure of UK financial regulation including the responsibilities of the main regulating bodies and the relationship between them:
>
> **Other regulators:** The UK Competition Commission, The Office of Fair Trading, The Information Commissioner and The Pensions Regulator
>
> **The relationships and coordination between:** Financial Conduct Authority, Prudential Regulation Authority, Financial Ombudsman Scheme (FOS), Financial Services Compensation Scheme (FSCS), Financial Policy Committee, Upper Tribunal (Tax and Chancery)

6.1 Introduction

We now look at a number of other bodies that have special roles in relation to UK financial services regulation.

6.2 The Competition Commission (CC)

The main statutory provisions on competition are to be found in the **2002 Enterprise Act**. UK competition rules are designed to ensure mergers and acquisitions are not going to result in uncompetitive practices or a **substantial lessening of competition**.

Competition investigations have a two-tier approach involving **Office of Fair Trading (OFT)** investigation followed by possible reference to the **Competition Commission (CC)** for a second-stage, in-depth investigation where necessary.

The **CC** also has a general function in ensuring that the operation of the regulatory regime set up under FSMA 2000 and the exercise by the regulators of their powers under the Act cannot be considered anti-competitive and that there are no adverse effects on competition.

More specifically, the CC has the following two roles under FSMA 2000.

- The first role (under **s162** FSMA 2000) concerns the regulators' rules, guidance and statements of principle, which the **Office of Fair Trading (OFT)** is responsible for keeping under review.

- The second role (under **s306** FSMA 2000) relates to the regulatory provisions and practices of **Recognised Investment Exchanges** and **Recognised Clearing Houses**. The OFT is also required to keep these regulatory provisions and practices under review.

In both cases, the **OFT** (see below) must make a **report** if it considers that rules, guidance and principles, or regulatory provisions and practices, have a significantly adverse effect on competition. The OFT may also make a report if it considers that there is no such effect on competition.

Any such report made by the OFT must be sent to the CC. The **CC** must **investigate** the subject matter of the OFT's report. If that report concludes that there is a significant adverse effect on competition and the OFT has asked the CC to consider the report, the CC must make its own report, unless it considers – giving reasons – that no useful purpose would be served by a report.

If the CC makes a report and concludes that there is an adverse effect on competition, it must also state whether it considers that the effect is justified and, if not, state what action the Treasury ought to direct the regulators to take.

6.3 The Office of Fair Trading (OFT)

6.3.1 The role of the OFT

The **Office of Fair Trading (OFT)** has the goal of helping make markets work well for consumers. Markets work well, the OFT states, 'when fair-dealing businesses are in open and vigorous competition with each other for custom'.

The OFT offers advice, support and guidance to businesses on competition issues and on consumer legislation. It also seeks to promote good practice in business by granting 'approved status' to Consumer Codes of Practice meeting set criteria. The OFT pursues businesses that rig prices or use unfair terms in contracts.

Under the **Control of Misleading Advertising Regulations**, the OFT works with bodies including the Advertising Standards Authority in exercising its powers to seek injunctions to stop advertising that is deceptive or misleading.

The OFT also currently regulates the consumer credit market with the aim of ensuring fair dealing by businesses in the market (but see below on future changes). It operates a **licensing system** through which checks are carried out on consumer credit businesses and it issues guidelines on how the law is enforced.

6.3.2 The OFT and the FCA and PRA

The OFT has specific responsibilities under FSMA 2000.

It is part of the role of the OFT to keep under review the activities and rules of the regulators with respect to competition issues.

If the OFT believes that regulatory rules will impact adversely on competition, then it will report this to the FCA, the Treasury and the **Competition Commission (CC)** (see above).

A **Memorandum of Understanding (MOU)** covers procedures in areas of common interest between the OFT and the FCA and PRA, to foster co-operation and to avoid duplication.

6.3.3 Changes to consumer credit regulation

The Government has announced that the **regulation of the consumer credit market** will be transferred from the OFT to the FCA on 1 April 2014.

The regulator plans to work with consumers, the industry and Government to develop proposals for effective regulation that helps the market to work well and seeks to ensure fair treatment for consumers. Proposals include an interim permission for OFT licence holders to continue to carry on regulated consumer credit activities.

6.4 Financial Ombudsman Service (FOS)

The **Financial Ombudsman Service (FOS)** will consider complaints against the activities of an authorised firm, including its appointed representatives, for an act or omission in carrying out any of the firm's regulated activities together with any ancillary activities that firm carries out. Complainants are expected to try to resolve complaints with the firm before referring the complaint to the FOS.

- The FOS is an independent body set up as a limited company under the FSMA 2000.
- The chairman and board of directors of the FOS are appointed by the FCA. The terms of the appointments must ensure their independence from the FCA.
- The FCA requires an annual report from the FOS on the scheme.
- The FOS has some power to make rules. Any rules that the FOS makes must be approved by the FCA.

6.5 Financial Services Compensation Scheme (FSCS)

While a customer who believes that they have been poorly advised may seek compensation through a ruling by the FOS to make good their loss, when a financial services firm gets into financial trouble and fails, compensation within specified limits is made available by the **Financial Services Compensation Scheme (FSCS)**, which is set up under FSMA 2000.

Similarly to the FOS, the chairman and board of directors of the FSCS are appointed by the FCA. The terms of the board's appointment are designed to ensure their independence from the FCA. The FSCS is required to make a report to the FCA annually.

6.6 The Information Commissioner

The **Information Commissioner's Office (ICO)** is an independent authority set up to uphold information rights in the public interest, promoting openness by public bodies and data privacy for individuals.

The ICO administers the provisions of the **Data Protection Act 1998** (which we return to later in this Study Text) and the Freedom of Information Act 2000.

The **Freedom of Information Act 2000** enables a public right to access information held by public authorities. Under this Act, public authorities are required to publish certain information about their activities. Members of the public may submit requests for information under the Act.

6.7 The Pensions Regulator

The **Pensions Regulator** is the regulatory body for **work-based pension schemes** in the UK. A work-based pension scheme is a scheme that an employer makes available to employees. This includes all occupational schemes, as well as stakeholder and personal pension schemes where employees have direct payment arrangements.

The Pensions Regulator has a defined set of statutory objectives, and wide powers to investigate schemes and to take action where necessary. The Regulator takes a proactive, risk-focused approach to regulation.

The **Pensions Act 2004** gave the Pensions Regulator the following objectives:

- To protect the benefits of members of work-based pension schemes
- To promote good administration of work-based pension schemes
- To reduce the risk of situations arising that may lead to claims for compensation from the **Pension Protection Fund (PPF)**

6.8 The Tax and Chancery Chamber of the Upper Tribunal

FSMA 2000 made provision for an independent body accountable to the **Ministry of Justice** (previously the Department for Constitutional Affairs). This body was established under the Financial Services and Markets Tribunal Rules 2001. It was known as the Financial Services and Markets Tribunal until the FSMT was abolished and its functions transferred to the **Tax and Chancery Chamber of the Upper Tribunal (TCCUT)** with effect from 6 April 2010, as part of a wider re-organisation of the tribunal system.

TCCUT has a wider role than just FCA and PRA decision cases. TCCUT is a Superior Court of Record with UK-wide jurisdiction in tax cases and references as well as against decisions of the financial services regulators. TCCUT has jurisdiction over charity cases in England and Wales. TCCUT also has jurisdiction against decisions of the **Pensions Regulator**, in England, Wales and Scotland. The chamber also has the power of judicial review in certain instances.

TCCUT can provide for a re-hearing of FCA and PRA enforcement and authorisation cases where the firm or individual and the relevant regulator have not been able to agree the outcome. If a firm or individual receives a Decision Notice or Supervisory Notice (which we explain later) or is refused authorisation or approval (also explained more fully later), it may refer this to the Tribunal. The Tribunal will determine what appropriate action the regulator should take and, in doing so, can consider any new evidence which has come to light since the original decision was made.

7 THE FCA AND PRA HANDBOOKS

7.1 Primary and secondary legislation

FSMA 2000 – which is **primary legislation** – provides the overall framework of the regulatory system, with much of the detail being provided by **secondary legislation**. Both FSMA 2000 and the secondary legislation are drafted by **HM Treasury**.

Secondary legislation links into various sections of FSMA 2000, fleshing out the requirements. An example of this concerns the authorisation requirement. FSMA 2000 requires that any firm undertaking a **regulated activity** must be authorised or exempt from authorisation. While the routes that a firm may follow to obtain authorisation are contained in FSMA 2000, the meaning of the term 'regulated activity' and the exemptions are found in secondary legislation – namely the **Regulated Activities Order**.

7.2 The FCA and PRA Handbooks

The principles, rules and regulations made by the regulators and to which a firm must adhere are found in the **FCA Handbook** and the **PRA Handbook**. Even where standards are imposed by FSMA 2000 itself, such as in the case of market abuse and financial promotions, the regulatory handbooks provide additional requirements and guidance.

The FCA and PRA Handbooks have initially been created by splitting the FSA's Handbook between the PRA and one for the FCA. Most provisions in the FSA Handbook are being incorporated into the **PRA Handbook**, the **FCA Handbook**, or both, in line with each new regulator's set of responsibilities and objectives.

7.3 Types of provision in the FCA and PRA Handbooks

The FCA and PRA Handbooks contains a number of different kinds of provisions, indicated by letters as follows.

R	This indicates a **rule** and means that it places a binding duty on a firm.
E	This indicates an **evidential provision**. If a firm complies with an evidential provision, this will tend to establish compliance with the linked rule. If a firm breaches an evidential provision, this will tend to establish that a breach of the linked rule has occurred.
G	This indicates **guidance**, which is not binding on a firm but it is used to flesh out particular issues arising from rules.
D	The letter **D** indicates **directions** and **requirements** given under various powers conferred by FSMA 2000 and relevant statutory instruments. Directions and requirements are **binding** upon the persons or categories of person to whom they are addressed.
UK	The **UK** flag icon is used to indicate directly applicable, non-FCA/PRA, UK legislative material, such as Acts of Parliament and statutory instruments, regulations and orders. Cross-references to this material will use the letters UK.
EU	An **EU** flag icon indicates EU legislative material, such as EU Directives and directly applicable EU Regulations. Cross-references to this material will use the letters **EU**.
P	The letter **P** is used to indicate the **Statements of Principle for approved persons** made under s64 of FSMA 2000. The Statements of Principle are **binding** on approved persons.
C	The letter **C** is used for paragraphs made under s119(2)(b) FSMA 2000 which specify descriptions of behaviour that, in the opinion of the FCA, **do not amount to market abuse**. These descriptions are conclusive because such behaviour is to be taken, for the purposes of the Act, as not amounting to market abuse.

7.4 Handbook Guides and Regulatory Guides

Additional to the main sections and 'sourcebooks' within the FCA and PRA Handbooks, **Handbook Guides** point particular kinds of firm in the direction of material relevant to them in the Handbooks. Handbook Guides include guides for Energy Market Participants, for Oil Market Participants, and for Service Companies.

There are also **Regulatory Guides** on certain topics, including the Enforcement Guide, and the Perimeter Guidance Manual (PERG) which gives guidance about the circumstances in which authorisation is required or exempt person status is available.

7.5 Industry guidance

Industry Guidance includes Codes of Practice and similar Statements generated by **trade associations and professional bodies** to help their members understand and follow good practice in meeting regulatory requirements.

As well as not taking action against a person for behaviour that it considers to be in line with **guidance**, the regulators will similarly not take action that is in line with **other materials** published by the regulators in support of the Handbooks or **regulator-confirmed Industry Guidance** which were current at the time of the behaviour in question.

However, as **Industry Guidance** is not mandatory (and is one way, but not the only way, to comply with requirements), the regulators do not presume that because firms are not complying with it they are not meeting regulatory requirements.

1: THE REGULATORY ENVIRONMENT

Chapter Roundup

- The Financial Services and Markets Act (FSMA) 2000 provides for a system of statutory regulation of the financial services industry. The Financial Services Authority (FSA) became the main statutory regulator for the financial services industry in 2001.

- The FSMA regulatory framework was introduced in response to various regulatory failures of the 1980s and 1990s, and replaced an earlier regime of 'self-regulating organisations'.

- The 'principles-based' approach to regulation implies that, rather than rely on detailed rules, the regulators expect firms to carry more responsibility in making their own judgement about how to apply regulatory principles to their business.

- Plans to re-structure the regulation of the UK financial services industry have resulted in the establishment of the Prudential Regulation Authority (PRA) and the Financial Conduct Authority (FCA) with effect from 1 April 2013. The PRA is the prudential regulator, responsible for ensuring the safe operation of deposit-taking institutions as well as insurers, investment banks and some other institutions. The FCA will be responsible for consumer protection in financial services, the regulation of conduct of business (including in firms regulated by the PRA) and market conduct.

- The objectives of the FCA and the PRA are set out in FSMA 2000, as amended by the Financial Services Act 2012. The FCA is responsible for both conduct and prudential regulation for those firms that are not subject to dual regulation.

- The role of the Bank of England has expanded following the abolition of the FSA and the 2013 re-organisation of the framework of regulation of the UK financial services industry. The Financial Policy Committee is a committee of the Bank.

- The regulators (the FCA and PRA) have wide powers, including approval of individuals to perform controlled functions, and authorisation of firms. The regulators can issue rules and codes of conduct, can investigate authorised firms or approved persons, and can take discipline and enforcement action.

- The Principles for Businesses (PRIN) state firms' fundamental obligations under the regulatory system, and require honest, fair and professional conduct from firms. The FCA emphasises the principle of Treating Customers Fairly (TCF), and expects firms to ensure that a number of desirable consumer outcomes are achieved in relation to TCF.

- Statements of Principle apply generally to all approved persons (ie relevant employees of regulated firms) when they are performing a controlled function. The Code of Practice for Approved Persons sets out types of conduct breaching the Statements of Principle.

- The Chartered Institute for Securities and Investment's Code of Conduct includes eight core Principles. If a member encounters a conflict of interest (CISI Principle 5), then the member may decide to decline to act.

- The SYSC manual encourages directors and senior managers of authorised firms to take appropriate responsibility for their firm's arrangements and to ensure they know their obligations.

- You should understand the role of these other bodies and agencies: HM Treasury, the Competition Commission, the Office of Fair Trading, the Information Commissioner, the Pensions Regulator, the Financial Ombudsman Service, the Financial Services Compensation Scheme, and the Upper Tribunal (Tax and Chancery).

- The FCA and PRA Handbooks contain detailed rules which authorised firms must abide by when conducting business. In addition to binding Rules, the Handbooks contains Evidential Provisions, and non-binding Guidance.

Test Your Knowledge

Check your knowledge of the chapter here, without referring back to the text.

1.	What is the strategic objective of the FCA?	
2.	What are the operational objectives of the FCA?	<ul><li></li><li></li><li></li></ul>
3.	What is the general objective of the PRA?	
4.	List six of the regulators' Principles for Businesses.	<ul><li></li><li></li><li></li></ul> <ul><li></li><li></li><li></li></ul>
5.	'Section 150 FSMA 2000 creates a right of action in damages for a private person who suffers loss from contravention of a rule or principle by an authorised firm.' Is this statement True or False?	
6.	Give an example of what is meant by an 'outcomes-focused' approach to regulation.	
7.	Which Statements of Principle apply to all approved persons? (State the title of each one.)	

1: THE REGULATORY ENVIRONMENT

8.	Which four parties should a CISI member approach if they find themselves in a position which might require them to contravene the CISI Principles?	<ul><li></li><li></li><li></li><li></li></ul>
9.	What body hears tax cases as well as cases relating to decisions of the FCA and PRA, and of the Pensions Regulator?	
10.	Which of the following letters indicating types of provision in the FCA and PRA Handbooks that are binding on firms: R, G, D, P?	

Test Your Knowledge: Answers

1. The strategic objective is 'Ensuring that the relevant markets function well'.

    (See Section 1.9)

2. The FCA's strategic objective is supported by three operational objectives:
    - Securing an appropriate degree of protection for consumers
    - Protecting and enhancing the integrity of the UK financial system
    - Promoting effective competition in the interests of consumers in the market for regulated financial services and for services provided by a recognised investment exchange

    (See Section 1.9)

3. The PRA's general objective is: 'Promoting the safety and soundness of PRA-authorised firms'.

    (See Section 1.7)

4. You could have listed any six of the following: Integrity, Skill, Care & Diligence, Management and Control, Financial Prudence, Market Conduct, Customers' Interests, Communications with Clients, Conflicts of Interest, Customers: Relationships of Trust, Clients' Assets, Relations with Regulators.

    (See Section 2.3)

5. False. A private person may sue a firm under s150 for the breach of a rule, but not of a Principle.

    (See Section 2.5)

6. An example of the developing emphasis on outcomes is found in the FCA's approach to the principle of treating customers fairly (TCF). The regulator has specified six TCF consumer outcomes against which firms are expected to measure their progress in meeting the TCF principle.

    (See Section 2.6)

7. The first four Statements of Principle apply to all approved persons. These are: Integrity; Skill, care and diligence; Proper standards of market conduct; Deal with the regulator in an open way.

    (See Section 3.2)

8. (1) Line manager; (2) Internal compliance department; (3) Firm's non-executive directors or audit committee; (4) the CISI.

    (See Section 4.2)

9. This is the Tax and Chancery Chamber of the Upper Tribunal, sometimes referred to simply as 'the Tribunal'.

    (See Section 6.8)

10. The correct answer is: R, D, and P. Rules, Directions, and Statements of Principle (P) are binding on firms. Guidance (G) is not binding.

    (See Section 7.3)

1: THE REGULATORY ENVIRONMENT

2 The Financial Services and Markets Act 2000

INTRODUCTION

The FSMA 2000 established the statutory role of the previous regulator, the FSA. The Financial Services Act 2012 has made amendments to the FSMA 2000 in order to set up the restructured regulatory system under the FCA and the PRA.

In this chapter, we look at the range of investments covered by the FSMA 2000, and at the range of activities that are regulated under the legislation. We explain more fully the regulators' enforcement powers which were referred to in the previous chapter.

As mentioned in the previous chapter, individuals carrying out 'controlled functions' are subject to the 'approved persons' regime, which is distinct from the process of authorisation of the firms in which such individuals work.

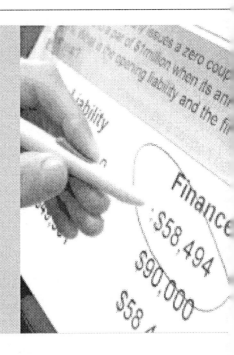

CHAPTER CONTENTS

	Page
1 Regulated and Prohibited Activities	40
2 Performance of Regulated Activities	43
3 Information Gathering and Investigations	48
4 Regulated Activities, Authorisation and Approval	49
Chapter Roundup	69
Test Your Knowledge	70

Learning Objectives

Regulated and prohibited activities

- **Know** the regulated and prohibited activities
  - Authorised persons
  - Exempt persons and FSMA Exemption Order 2001
  - Offences under the Act
  - Enforceability of agreements entered into with an unauthorised business
  - Defences available under the Act

- **Understand** the powers of the prohibition order in respect of the performance of regulated activities

Performance of regulated activities

- **Know** the role of the FCA and PRA enforcement division, the power of the FCA and PRA to make decisions by executive procedures and the role, scope and consequences of the Regulatory Decisions Committee's responsibility for decision-making

- **Know** the outcomes of the FCA's and PRA's statutory notices, the regulatory enforcement processes: warning, decision, supervisory and final notices and the firm's right to refer to the Tribunal

- **Know** the FCA's powers of intervention (products and financial promotions)

Information gathering and investigations

- **Know** the regulators' power to require information and to appoint persons to carry out investigations

Regulated activities

- **Know** the activities specified in Part II of the Regulated Activities Order

- **Know** the main exclusions from the need for authorisation under the FSMA 2000 (Regulated Activities Order)
  - Dealing as principal
  - Advice in newspapers
  - Trustees, nominees and personal representatives
  - Employee share schemes
  - Overseas persons

- **Know** the investments specified in Part III of the Regulated Activities Order

- **Know** the authorisation procedures for firms
  - The need for authorisation
  - The threshold conditions for authorisation

- **Know** the supervisory process
  - Purpose of supervision arrangements
  - Focus on a firm's senior management
  - Risk-based approach to regulation
  - Tools for supervision
  - Transaction reporting regime

- **Know** the approval processes for Approved Persons
  - The application process
  - The criteria for approval as an Approved Person

- **Understand** the FCA's and PRA's controlled functions: the five functional areas, the required functions, the four areas of significant influence functions, the requirement for FCA and PRA approval prior to performing the function

- **Know** the Training and Competence regime:
  - The application of the systems and control responsibilities in relation to the competence of employees
  - Assessing and maintaining competence, the examination requirements before starting activities, how firms must assess at the outset and at regular intervals the training needs of their employees, maintaining competence
  - Activities to which the T&C rules apply

- **Know** the legal and regulatory basis for whistleblowing

1 Regulated and Prohibited Activities

> **Learning objectives**
>
> **Know** the regulated and prohibited activities: authorised persons; exempt persons and FSMA Exemption Order 2001; offences under the Act; enforceability of agreements entered into with an unauthorised business; defences available under the Act
>
> **Understand** the powers of the prohibition order in respect of the performance of regulated activities

1.1 The general prohibition

Section 19 FSMA 2000 contains what is known as the **general prohibition**.

The general prohibition states that no person can carry on a regulated activity in the UK, nor purport to do so, unless they are either **authorised or exempt**.

The definition of person here includes both **companies and individuals**. The list of exemptions and exclusions are set out in the regulations. There is no right to apply for an exemption from s19 if you do not fall into the existing categories.

The sanctions for breaching s19 are fairly severe, namely: criminal sanctions, unenforceability of agreements, compensation, and actions by the regulator to restrain such activity.

Section 56 FSMA 2000 allows the relevant regulator to issue an Order to stop individuals from carrying out specified functions in relation to regulated activities within the investment industry. Such an Order is called a **Prohibition Order**.

Section 59 FSMA 2000 states that a person (ie, a member of staff at an authorised firm) cannot carry out a **controlled function** in a firm unless that **individual has been approved** by the relevant regulator.

1.2 Criminal sanctions and defence

Breach of the general prohibition is punishable in a court of law, subject to a maximum sentence of two years plus an unlimited fine.

It is a **defence** for a person to show that all reasonable precautions were taken and all due diligence exercised, to avoid committing the offence.

1.3 Unenforceable agreements

As a consequence of the general prohibition, an agreement made by an **unauthorised** firm will be **unenforceable** against the other party.

FSMA 2000 makes it clear that agreements are not illegal or invalid as a result of a contravention of the general prohibition: they are merely '**voidable**'. This ensures that the innocent party to the agreement may still be able to enforce the agreement against the other party, even though the performance may be a criminal offence.

1.4 Compensation

The innocent party will be entitled to recover **compensation** for any loss sustained if the agreement is made unenforceable.

1.5 Injunctions and restitution orders

The regulators may seek **injunctions** and **restitution orders** to restrain the contravention of the general prohibition and seek to remove the profits from offenders.

1.6 The requirement for authorisation

As stated above, no person can carry on a regulated activity in the UK, nor purport to do so, unless they are either **authorised** or **exempt**.

As mentioned earlier, the **Perimeter Guidance Manual (PERG)** in the FCA Handbook provides guidance about the circumstances in which authorisation is required, or exempt person status is available, including guidance on the activities which are regulated under FSMA 2000 and the exclusions which are available.

A firm will apply to either the FCA or the PRA, depending on the type of firm.

- **Dual-regulated firms** (banks and building societies, credit unions, insurers and some investment firms) are authorised by the PRA but only with FCA approval.
- **FCA-only regulated firms** (including independent financial advisers, investment exchanges, insurance brokers and fund managers) are authorised by the FCA.

The following decision chart indicates the questions to be asked in establishing **whether a firm needs to be authorised**.

Does My Firm Need Authorisation?

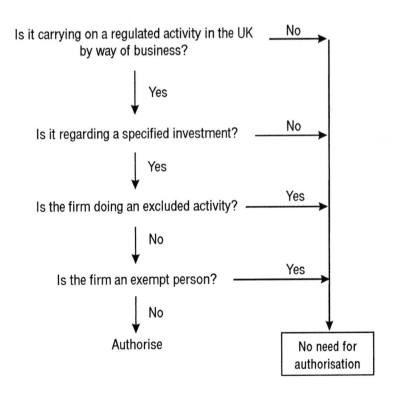

1.7 Exempt persons

The following are the types of person that are **exempt** from the requirement to seek authorisation under FSMA 2000.

- **Appointed representative**. In markets such as life assurance, the bulk of sales take place through self-employed individuals who act on behalf of the companies. As the companies do not employ them, if this exemption were not in place, such persons would need separate authorisation. The exemption removes them from the scope of authorisation so long as they act solely on behalf of one firm and that firm takes complete responsibility for their actions.

- **Members of professions**. Some of the investment business activities of certain members of professions, such as lawyers, accountants and actuaries enjoy an exemption for the requirement for authorisation. Member firms of **'Designated Professional Bodies' (DPBs)** – including the Institute of Chartered Accountants in England and Wales (ICAEW), the Law Society, the Institute of Actuaries, the Council for Licensed Conveyancers, and the Royal Institution of Chartered Surveyors – require authorisation if they recommend the purchase of specific investments such as pensions or listed company shares to clients, approve financial promotions or carry out corporate finance business. If the firms' activities are 'non-mainstream' investment business, only assisting clients in making investment decisions as part of other professional services, they are exempt from authorisation but must obtain a licence from the DPB, under which they are subject to a lighter form of regulation.

- **Certain persons listed in the Financial Services and Markets Act (Exemption) Order 2001**, including supranational bodies, municipal banks, local authorities, housing associations, the national grid, trade unions, the Treasury Taskforce, the English Tourist Board, government organisations (such as Bank of England, other central banks, and the International Monetary Fund and the UK's National Savings & Investments), enterprise schemes (ie bodies with the objective of promoting or disseminating information about enterprise). Charities and the Student Loans Company are also exempt in respect of deposit-taking activities. The Financial Services and Markets Act (Exemption) Order 2001 is written by HM Treasury under powers set out in s38 FSMA 2000.

- **Members of Lloyd's**. The requirement to seek authorisation is disapplied for members of Lloyd's writing insurance contracts. The Society of Lloyd's, however, is required to be authorised. This exemption covers **being** a Lloyd's member but does not cover the activities of **advising** on Lloyd's syndicate participation or **managing** underwriting activities.

- **Recognised Investment Exchanges (RIEs), Recognised Overseas Investment Exchanges (ROIEs)** and **Recognised Clearing Houses (RCHs)**. FSMA 2000 gives to the FCA the role of recognising, regulating and supervising investment exchanges (such as the London Stock Exchange, NYSE Liffe and the London Metal Exchange) and clearing houses (such as Euroclear UK & Ireland).

> **Exam tip**
>
> The word **APRIL** can be used to help learn the five types of exempt persons.
> **A**ppointed representatives
> **P**rofessional people, eg solicitors, accountants and actuaries
> **R**IE, ROIEs and RCHs
> **I**nstitutions which are exempt, eg the Bank of England
> **L**loyd's members

2 Performance of Regulated Activities

2.1 Regulatory Decisions Committee (RDC)

> **Learning objective**
>
> **Know** the role of the FCA and PRA enforcement divisions, the power of the FCA and PRA to make decisions by executive procedures and the role, scope and consequences of the Regulatory Decisions Committee's responsibility for decision-making

The relevant regulator's **Enforcement Division** will investigate when firms breach rules or the provisions of FSMA 2000. Enforcement staff prepare and recommend action in individual cases. For more significant decisions (called **statutory notice decisions**) the regulator passes the case to another body which is a separate Committee of the FCA, called the **Regulatory Decisions Committee (RDC)**.

The RDC will look at the case and decide whether or not to take action. This would cover the giving of fines, censures, restitution orders, and withdrawing, varying or refusing authorisation or approval. For less serious disciplinary actions, eg requesting the firm to provide reports, the regulator may act itself under its '**executive procedures**'.

The RDC is appointed by the FCA Board to exercise certain regulatory powers on its behalf. It is accountable to the board of the FCA for the decisions. However, the RDC is outside the regulator's management structure and, apart from the Chairman of the RDC, none of the RDC's members are FCA employees. The RDC members comprise practitioners and suitable individuals representing the public interest.

If the RDC decide to take action:

- A **Warning Notice** will be sent, containing details of the proposed action. The person concerned then has access to the material which the regulator is relying on and may make **oral or written representations** to the RDC. The FCA has a new power under the **Financial Services Act 2012** to **publish** Warning Notices, after consulting the person concerned – thus announcing that they have begun disciplinary action against a firm or an individual.

- The RDC will then issue a **Decision Notice** detailing the reasons for the decision, proposed sanction and a notice of the right to refer the matter to the Tax and Chancery Chamber of the Upper Tribunal (TCCUT), which undertakes a complete rehearing of the case.

- When a decision notice is accepted, or appeals finalised, a **Final Notice** is sent to the person.

A Final Notice only contains FCA/RDC/Tribunal discipline, not any disciplinary action the firm has taken itself.

Under Part V of FSMA 2000, the regulator must commence disciplinary action within **two years** of first being aware of the misconduct.

2.2 Regulatory enforcement

> **Learning objectives**
>
> **Know** the outcomes of the FCA's and PRA's statutory notices, and the regulatory enforcement process: warning, decision, supervisory and final notices
>
> **Know** the firm's right to refer to the Tribunal

The regulators must be proportionate in their use of enforcement measures: 'the punishment must fit the crime'. The disciplinary process has been designed to ensure that it is compliant with human rights legislation. Therefore, while the regulator's staff will investigate the matter and decide whether they feel enforcement action is appropriate, they will not take the final decision on matters of such regulatory significance.

The regulator can take decisions under its own **executive procedures** for matters of lesser regulatory impact to the firms, such as imposing a requirement on a firm to submit regular reports covering activities such a trading, complaints or management accounts. As we have seen, more significant decisions are made by the **RDC** (Regulatory Decisions Committee).

2.3 Statutory notices

Under FSMA 2000, the **statutory notices** that may be issued include Warning Notices, Decision Notices and Supervisory Notices. In addition to these Statutory Notices, there are other related notices.

- **Warning notice**: gives the recipient details about action the regulator or RDC proposes to take and the recipient's right to make representations.

- **Decision notice**: gives the recipient details of the action the regulator or RDC has decided to take subject to the RDC going through its formal procedures. The regulator is permitted to publish decision notices. Their approach is to publish the decision notice only if the person refers the matter to the Tribunal, unless there is a compelling reason to publish before that.

- **Further decision notice**: gives the recipient details of different action the regulator or RDC has decided to take subsequent to giving the original Decision Notice. This can only be given where the recipient consents.

- **Supervisory notice**: gives the recipient details about action the regulator or RDC has taken or proposes to take, normally with immediate effect (prior to formal procedures). In the Decision Procedure and Penalties Manual (DEPP), the supervisory notice about a matter first given to the recipient is referred to as the **first supervisory notice** and the supervisory notice given after consideration of any representations is referred to as the **second supervisory notice**.

2.4 Non-statutory notices

- **Notice of discontinuance**: is issued where proceedings set out in a decision or warning notice are being discontinued.

- **Final notice**: sets out the terms of the action the regulator or RDC has decided to take and the date it takes effect from.

2.5 Factors influencing enforcement action

In determining whether or not to take enforcement action, the relevant regulator will consider the full circumstances of the case. Some of the factors they may consider are as follows.

- The **nature and seriousness** of the breach, including:
    - Whether the breach was deliberate or reckless
    - Whether the breach reveals serious or systemic weaknesses of the firm's management systems or internal controls of a firm
    - The loss or risk of loss to consumers and market users

- The **conduct** of the firm or approved person after the breach, including:
    - How quickly, effectively, and completely, the firm or approved person brought the breach to the attention of the regulator

- Any remedial steps the firm or approved person has taken since the breach, eg compensating consumers and any internal disciplinary action
- The previous regulatory record of the firm

In certain cases, the regulator may determine that it is not appropriate to bring formal enforcement proceedings, for example, if the conduct is minor or where full remedial action was taken by the firm or approved person themselves (although these facts are not necessarily conclusive that the regulator will not bring formal proceedings).

If the regulator think it would be beneficial for the approved person or firm to know that they were close to being the subject of formal proceedings, then the Authority can issue a **Private Warning**, which will:

- State that, while the regulator has cause for concern, it does not intend to take formal proceedings
- Form part of the firm or approved person's compliance history and may be relevant when determining future proceedings
- Ask the recipient to acknowledge receipt and to comment on the warning if they so wish

2.6 Right to refer to TCCUT

A person who receives a Decision Notice or Supervisory Notice has the right to refer the decision to the **Tribunal (TCCUT)**.

The Tribunal is not bound by earlier proceedings. Iit can increase or reduce the penalty and can look at new evidence.

2.7 Regulatory enforcement powers

2.7.1 Overview

The regulator may discipline authorised firms or approved persons for acts of misconduct in order to pursue its regulatory objectives. The detail is contained in the **Enforcement Guide**. We now examine various enforcement measures that can be applied against approved persons and authorised firms.

2.7.2 Public censure and statements of misconduct

The relevant regulator may issue a public censure on a firm – 'naming and shaming' – where the firm has contravened a requirement imposed under FSMA 2000. The regulator may issue a public statement of misconduct to an approved person where the approved person is guilty of **'misconduct'**. Misconduct means breaching a Statement of Principle or being knowingly concerned in the contravention of a regulatory requirement by their firm. The regulator will issue a **Warning Notice** of its intention to censure in this way.

In determining whether to issue a censure/statement of misconduct or give a financial penalty, the regulator will look at all the relevant circumstances, including:

- Whether the accused made a profit or avoided a loss as a result of the misconduct – if so, a financial penalty may be more appropriate
- Whether the accused has admitted the breach, co-operated with the regulator or compensated consumers – if so a censure/statement of misconduct may be more appropriate
- The accused's disciplinary record/compliance history – a poor record or history may make a financial penalty more appropriate

More serious breaches are more likely to receive a financial penalty.

2: THE FINANCIAL SERVICES AND MARKETS ACT 2000

2.7.3 Financial penalties – fines

The regulator will impose a financial penalty on a firm where the firm has contravened a requirement imposed under FSMA 2000. The regulator may impose a financial penalty on an approved person where the approved person is guilty of 'misconduct' (as defined earlier). The regulator can also impose a financial penalty on any person who has committed market abuse and also on an applicant for listing or an issuer of listed securities where the UKLA listing rules have been breached. In determining the **size of the penalty**, the regulator must have regard to:

- The seriousness of the misconduct
- The extent to which the misconduct was deliberate or reckless
- Whether the person on whom the penalty is to be imposed is an individual

To impose a financial penalty, the regulator must give the individual a **Warning Notice** followed by a **Decision Notice** and a **Final Notice** and the individual must be able to refer the matter to the Tribunal (TCCUT). Financial penalties are normally published via a press release unless it would be unfair on the person to whom the penalty is imposed or prejudicial to the interests of consumers.

2.7.4 Restitution order/redress

Where a person (whether authorised or not) has breached a relevant requirement the regulators have powers to apply to the court to require that person to effect restitution on the affected consumers (ie, **restore them to the pre-breach situation**). In determining whether to exercise its powers, the regulator will have regard to the circumstances of the case and also other facts, including other ways the consumer might get redress and whether it would be more effective or cost effective for the regulator to require redress.

In addition to the enforcement measures mentioned above, the regulator can take the following **preventative or remedial action**.

2.7.5 Cancellation or variation of authorisation or approval

Under FSMA 2000, the regulators may **vary** a **Part 4A permission** (permission to carry out specific regulated activities) where:

- The firm is failing or likely to fail to meet the threshold conditions (see later in this Chapter) for one or more of the regulated activities in respect of which it has Part 4A permission
- The firm has not carried out a regulated activity for which it has a Part 4A permission for at least 12 months, or
- It is desirable to protect consumers

The regulator will consider **cancelling** a firm's Part 4A permission where:

- It has very serious concerns about a firm or the way its business has been conducted, or
- The firm's regulated activities have come to an end and it has not applied for its permissions to be cancelled

Applications for **variations or cancellations of permission** are dealt with as follows.

- A **dual-regulated firm** must apply to the PRA. The PRA may determine an application to vary permission only with the FCA's consent. In making its decision, the FCA may make reasonable requests for additional information from the firm. The PRA must consult the FCA in determining an application to cancel a permission.

- An **FCA-only regulated firm** will apply to the FCA. If the applicant firm is part of a group that includes a dual-regulated firm, the FCA must consult the PRA in making its decision.

As we have seen and as we shall explain in more detail later in this chapter, **individuals** must be **approved** by the regulator to perform specified **controlled functions** – a different process from the **authorisation** of a **firm**.

- Approval may be removed if the individual is no longer fit and proper to conduct that controlled function. To withdraw approval, the regulator must give the individual a Warning Notice followed by a Decision Notice and the individual must be able to refer the matter to the Tribunal.

- In deciding whether to withdraw approval, the regulator will take into account the controlled functions being performed and a variety of factors including: qualifications and training; the fitness and propriety of the individual (eg honesty, integrity, reputation, competence, capability, financial soundness); and whether the approved person has breached a statement of principle or been involved in his firm breaching a rule. The regulator will also consider the severity of the risk posed to consumers and confidence in the financial system and look at the individual's disciplinary record. Final notices of withdrawal of approval are normally published unless this would prejudice the interests of consumers.

2.7.6 Prohibition orders

> **Learning objective**
> **Understand** the FCA's actions in respect of prohibition orders and actions for damages

As stated earlier in this Chapter, Section 56 FSMA 2000 allows the FCA to issue a **Prohibition Order** to ban individuals from carrying out specified functions in relation to regulated activities within the investment industry. A **Prohibition Order** may be issued in respect of anyone whether they are an **approved person** or not: such an order could be imposed on a trader, a director, an IT staff member or a secretary, for example. The PRA can issue a Prohibition Order in respect of PRA-regulated activities or PRA-authorised firms.

The regulator will exercise its power to make a Prohibition Order where it determines that the individual represents a risk to consumers or confidence in the market generally and is not fit and proper to carry out that function. The order may relate to specified regulated activities or to the activities done by a particular firm or firms. To issue a Prohibition Order, the Authority must give the individual a Warning Notice followed by a Decision Notice and the individual must be able to refer the matter to the Tribunal.

If the regulator wishes to discipline an approved person, they can use either the withdrawal of approval route or issue a Prohibition Order. A Prohibition Order is much wider than the withdrawal of approval. The regulator will only issue a Prohibition Order if the degree of risk to consumers or confidence in the financial system cannot be addressed by simply withdrawing approval for the relevant controlled function.

In deciding whether to make a Prohibition Order, the regulator will look at the same type of factors as for the withdrawal of approval mentioned above. An unapproved person breaching a Prohibition Order is subject to a **maximum fine of £5,000** (also known as a **level 5 fine**) in the Magistrates Court. Note that this is a different penalty from the criminal penalties relating to the general prohibition (s19 FSMA 2000) described earlier.

Final notices of the issue of Prohibition Orders are normally **published** on the regulator's website.

2.8 FCA intervention powers

> **Learning objective**
> **Know** the FCA's powers of intervention (products and financial promotions)

2.8.1 Product intervention

An initiative of the FSA that will be taken forward by the FCA concerns identifying consumer detriment problems at an earlier stage through **product intervention**.

The FCA's product intervention power gives it the 'flexibility to intervene quickly and decisively' where it considers that a product or product feature is likely to result in significant consumer detriment. The FCA will seek to deal with the root of the problem, rather than reacting to the effects, when it is already too late.

In a December 2012 Consultation Paper, the regulator gave examples of some of the types of situation in which the FCA may choose to make temporary product intervention rules.

Situations that may trigger temporary rules being made: examples

- Where a product is in serious danger of being sold to the wrong customers, for instance where complex or niche products are sold to the mass market
- Where a non-essential feature of a product seems to be causing serious problems for consumers
- Where a product is inherently flawed

2.8.2 Financial promotions power

The FCA also has a new **power** under the Financial Services Act 2012 to ban misleading advertising (**'financial promotions'**). The regulator will be able to give a **direction** to firms requiring the firm immediately to withdraw or to modify promotions which it deems to be misleading, and to publish such decisions. We return to this topic in Chapter 4 of this Study Text when we consider financial promotions in more detail.

3 INFORMATION GATHERING AND INVESTIGATIONS

> **Learning objective**
>
> **Know** the regulators' power to require information and to appoint persons to carry out investigations

Under **s165** FSMA 2000, the regulators may, by written notice, require an authorised firm (or any person connected with it) or certain other persons (eg RIEs) to produce specified information or documents, which it reasonably requires.

The regulator may:

- Require information or documents to be provided within a specified, reasonable timescale and at a specified place
- Require that the information provided is verified and documents are authenticated
- Require access to an authorised firm's premises on demand: **no notice** need be given

The regulator may also obtain a report from a skilled person (such as an accountant).

The Authority may launch an **investigation** on a number of grounds, including:

- (For an authorised firm) where it has good reason to do so
- Where any person has contravened specific provisions of the regulatory regime (eg market abuse)
- At the request of an overseas regulator

While the regulator will normally give the subject of the investigation written notice, it can commence an investigation without doing this if it feels that the provision of the notice may result in the investigation being frustrated.

During the course of an investigation, there is no automatic requirement that the firm or an approved person cease trading.

FSMA 2000 gives sweeping powers to investigators. Generally, the regulator can also require a person under investigation or any connected person to attend at a specified time and place for questioning. The regulator may also require a person to **produce documents** (of which the investigator may take copies only).

Failure to co-operate with an investigator without reasonable excuse is a **criminal offence**. The regulator may also take action themselves such as increasing the severity of the sanction for the original breach. This effectively removes a person's right to silence. In order to ensure that the regime is compliant with human rights legislation, such answers will not be admissible in criminal or market abuse proceedings.

4 REGULATED ACTIVITIES, AUTHORISATION AND APPROVAL

4.1 List of activities regulated

> **Learning objective**
>
> **Know** the activities specified in Part II by the Regulated Activities Order

What range of activities are **regulated activities**? The activities regulated by FSMA 2000 are set out in the **Regulated Activities Order** (as amended).

Regulated activities

- **Accepting deposits.** These must be accepted by way of business to be covered.
- **Issuing electronic money.** Some banks and building societies issue 'e-money' which is a form of electronic money that can be used (like notes and coins) to pay for goods and services.
- **Effecting or carrying out contracts of insurance as principal.** After date 'N2' (30 November 2001), the regulator took responsibility for regulating all insurers for capital adequacy purposes and life insurance firms for Conduct of Business Rules. Since January 2005, the regulator has regulated the sales and administration of general insurance as well as life insurance.
- **Dealing in investments as principal or agent.** This covers buying, selling, subscribing for or underwriting investments.
- **Arranging deals in investments.** This covers making, offering or agreeing to make any arrangements with a view to another person buying, selling, subscribing for or underwriting investments.
- **Arranging regulated mortgage contracts.** This covers most mortgages, but generally does not cover buy-to-let or second charge loans.
- **Arranging home reversion plans.** Home reversion plans are one of two types of equity release product, the other being lifetime mortgages.
- **Arranging home purchase plans.** A home purchase plan serves the same purpose as a normal mortgage, in that it provides consumers with finance to buying a home. But it is structured in a way that makes it acceptable under Islamic law. As interest is contrary to Islamic law, a home purchase plan is in essence a sale and lease arrangement. The plan provider buys the property, which is then sold to the home purchaser by instalments.

- **Operating a multilateral trading facility (MTF).** This is a system which may be operated by an investment firm that enables parties, who might typically be retail investors or other investment firms, to buy and sell financial instruments.

> **MTFs** may be crossing networks or matching engines that are operated by an investment firm or a market operator. Instruments traded on a MTF may include shares, bonds and derivatives. The implementation of the Markets in Financial Instruments Directive (MiFID) created a wave of competition in equities trading, as the new alternative equities trading platforms known as MTFs were created to challenge traditional stock exchanges. MTFs in Europe include platforms such as Turquoise, Chi-X and BATS Europe. MTFs may operate as so-called dark pools, where buyers and sellers are matched anonymously. Under MiFID rules, these dark pools are not required to post prices publicly before trades take place. MiFID also provides for the operators of MTFs to passport their services across borders.

- **Managing investments.** Managing investments belonging to another person where there is exercise of discretion by the manager.
- **Assisting in the administration and performance of a contract of insurance** (see above).
- **Safeguarding and administering investments** or arranging such activities.
- **Sending dematerialised instructions.** This relates to the use of computer-based systems for giving instructions for investments to be transferred.
- **Establishing a collective investment scheme.** This would include the roles of the trustee and the depository of schemes.

    Sections 235 and 236 FSMA 2000 define 'Collective Investment Schemes' to mean arrangements regarding property of any description where the participants and profits or income are pooled and the property in the scheme is managed by an operator.

- **Establishing, operating or winding-up a personal pension scheme or a stakeholder pension scheme.** Personal pension schemes include Self-Invested Personal Pensions (SIPPs), as their name implies. A stakeholder pension scheme follows similar rules to a personal pension plan, with caps on charges in addition.
- **Advising on investments.**
- **Advising on regulated mortgage contracts.**
- **Advising on regulated home reversion plans.**
- **Advising on regulated home purchase plans.**
- **Lloyd's market activities.** Lloyd's is the UK's largest insurance market.
- **Entering funeral plan contracts.**
- **Entering into and administering a regulated mortgage contract.** Initially, the regulator regulated mortgage lending only, but since 31 October 2004 the regulator has regulated mortgage advice and administration in addition to mortgage lending.
- **Entering into and administering a home reversion plan.**
- **Entering into and administering a home purchase plan.**
- **Agreeing to carry on most regulated activities.** This is itself a regulated activity and so a firm must get the appropriate authorisation before agreeing to do business such as dealing or arranging for clients.

As you can see from the above list, the activities regulated cover the investment industry, banking, insurance and mortgage lending industries, and Lloyd's.

4.2 Activities carried on 'by way of business'

Note that the regulated activity must be carried on **'by way of business'** for the regulations to apply. Whether something is carried on by way of business is, ultimately, a question of judgement: in general terms it will depend on the degree of continuity and profit. HM Treasury has also (via secondary legislation) made explicit provisions for certain activities, such as accepting deposits. This will not be regarded as carried on by way of business if a person does not hold himself out as doing so on a day-to-day basis (that is, he only accepts deposits on particular occasions). An example of this would be a car salesman accepting a down payment on the purchase of a car.

4.3 Excluded activities

> **Learning objective**
>
> **Know** the main exclusions from the need for authorisation under the FSMA 2000 (Regulated Activities Order)

As set out in the Regulated Activities Order and reiterated in PERG, the following activities are **excluded** from the requirement for authorisation.

- **Dealing as principal** where the person is not holding themselves out to the market as willing to deal. The requirement to seek authorisation does not apply to the personal dealings of unauthorised individuals for their own account, ie, as customers of an authorised firm. It would also exclude companies issuing their own shares.

- **Trustees, nominees and personal representatives**. These persons, so long as they do not hold themselves out to the general public as providing the service and are not separately remunerated for the regulated activity, are excluded from the requirement to seek authorisation.

- **Employee share schemes**. This exclusion applies to activities which further an employee share scheme.

- **Media**, eg TV, radio and newspapers. Many newspapers and other media give investment advice. However, provided this is not the primary purpose of the newspaper, then under the exceptions granted within FSMA 2000, it need not seek formal authorisation. On the other hand, the publication of '**tip sheets**' (written recommendations of investments) will require authorisation.

- **Overseas persons**. Overseas persons are firms which do not carry on regulated activity from a permanent place within the UK. This exception covers two broad categories: first, where the activity requires the direct involvement of an authorised or exempt firm and, second, where the activity is carried on as a result of an unsolicited approach by a UK individual. Thus, if a UK individual asks a fund manager in Tokyo to buy a portfolio of Asian equities for them, the Japanese firm does not need to be authorised under FSMA 2000.

> **Exam tip**
>
> The word **DEMOTE** can help you to learn the five excluded activities.
>
> **D**ealing as principal, where the person is not holding themselves out to the market as willing to deal
> **E**mployee share schemes
> **M**edia
> **O**verseas persons
> **T**rustees
> Nomin**E**es and personal representatives

4.4 Specified investments

> **Learning objective**
> **Know** the investments specified in Part III of the Regulated Activities Order

Only activities relating to **specified investments** are covered by FSMA 2000. Specified investments are also defined in the **Regulated Activities Order** (as amended).

Specified investments

- **Deposits.** Simply defined, this is a sum of money paid by one person to another under the terms that it will be repaid on a specified event (eg on demand).
- **Electronic money.** This is defined as monetary value, as represented by a claim on the issuer, which is stored on an electronic device, is issued on receipt of funds and is accepted as a means of payment by persons other than the issuer.
- **Rights under a contract of insurance.** Included in this category are general insurance contracts (such as motor insurance, accident or sickness), long-term insurance contracts (such as life and annuity) and other insurance contracts (such as funeral expense contracts).
- **Shares** or stock in the capital of a company wherever the company is based.
- **Debentures, loan stock and similar instruments,** eg certificate of deposit, Treasury bills of exchange, floating rate notes, bulldog bonds and unsecured loan stock (but not cheques or other bill of exchange, banker's drafts, letters of credit, trade bills or Premium Bonds).
- **Government and public securities,** eg gilts, US Treasury bonds (not National Savings & Investments products, such as Premium Bonds and Savings Certificates).
- **Warrants.** A warrant gives the right to buy a new share in a company.
- **Certificates representing certain securities,** eg American Depository Receipts.
- **Units in a Collective Investment Scheme** including shares in, or securities of, an Open-Ended Investment Company (OEIC). A collective investment scheme is a specified investment whatever underlying property the scheme invests in.
- **Rights under a personal pension scheme or a stakeholder pension scheme.** These are pension plans which are not employment-based (occupational) schemes. As indicated above, a SIPP is a personal pension scheme.
- **Options** to acquire or dispose of any specified investment or currencies, gold, silver, platinum or palladium.
- **Futures** on anything for investment purposes. This differs from the treatment of options as it will cover all futures regardless of the underlying investment, provided it is for investment purposes.

The definition of 'investment purposes' is complex. In general terms, any futures contract traded either on an exchange, or in an over-the-counter market or form similar to that traded on an exchange, will constitute an investment. The type of future, in effect, excluded by this definition would be a short-term contract between a producer and a consumer of a good to purchase that good in the future, eg a wheat buyer buying from a farmer. This can sometimes be referred to as a 'commercial purpose future'.

> **Exam tip**
> As a rule of thumb, unless the examiner indicates otherwise, you should assume that a future *is* for investment purposes.

- **Contracts for differences (CfDs).** A CfD is a contract whose price tracks the price of an underlying asset, while the CfD holder does not take ownership of the asset. The underlying asset might be a company's shares, a bond, a currency, a commodity or an index. Investors can use CfDs to take a short position – and thus gain from price declines, but lose if the price rises.
- **Lloyd's syndicate capacity and syndicate membership.** Lloyd's is an insurance institution specialising in risks such as aviation and marine insurance. Insurance is provided by members and syndicates.
- **Rights under a funeral plan contract.** These are contracts whereby someone pays for their funeral before their death.
- **Rights under a regulated mortgage contract.** Note that not all mortgages are covered, only regulated mortgages. In a regulated mortgage the loan is secured by a first legal mortgage or property located in the UK, which will be occupied (at least 40% of the time) by the borrower or their family.
- **Rights under a home reversion plan.**
- **Rights under a home purchase plan.**
- **Rights to or interests in anything that is a specified investment listed** (excluding 'Rights under regulated mortgage contracts'). 'Repos' (sale and repurchase agreements) in relation to specified investments (eg a government bond) are specified investments.

Spot currency ('forex') trades, general loans (eg car loans), property deals and National Savings & Investments products are *not* specified investments.

When applying for authorisation to carry out a regulated activity regarding a specified investment, the firm will specify on the application form which regulated activities relating to which specified investments it wishes to conduct.

4.5 Authorisation routes

> **Learning objective**
>
> **Know** the authorisation procedure for firms: the need for authorisation; the threshold conditions for authorisation

FSMA 2000 has created a single authorisation regime for the regulated activities within its scope. This contrasts with the previous financial services regulation arrangements, which contained a variety of separate regulatory regimes.

A firm may be authorised by one of two main routes:

- Authorisation by the FCA or PRA
- Passporting

The concept of a '**passport**' enables a firm to conduct business throughout the EEA. Passporting is discussed in more detail in Chapter 3 of this Study Text.

4.6 Authorisation by the regulators

By far the most common route to authorisation is to obtain permission from one of the regulators to carry out one or more regulated activities.

As explained earlier, a firm will apply to either the FCA or the PRA, depending on the type of firm.

- **Dual-regulated firms** are authorised by the PRA, with FCA approval
- **FCA-only regulated firms** are authorised by the FCA

The permission that a firm receives will play a crucial role in defining the firm's business scope. This permission is referred to as **Part 4A permission** as it is set out in Part 4A of FSMA 2000 (as amended by the Financial Services Act 2012).

Where a firm obtains permission to do one or more regulated activities, it is then authorised to undertake those activities. In the application, the applicant must set out which regulated activities and specified investments it requires permission for. The permission will set out what activities and investments are covered and any limitations and requirements that the regulator wishes to impose.

It is not a criminal offence for a firm to go beyond its permission but doing so may give rise to claims from consumers. Furthermore, the regulators will be able to use the full range of regulatory sanctions, such as cancelling or varying permission.

4.7 Threshold conditions

4.7.1 Introduction

Before it grants permission, the relevant regulator must be satisfied that the firm is **fit and proper**. In accordance with FSMA 2000, the firm must meet and continue to satisfy the '**threshold conditions**' for the activity concerned in order to be deemed fit and proper.

The **FCA and the PRA** each have their own set of threshold conditions, but a number of the conditions are common to both regulators. Each regulator must ensure that a firm meets that regulator's threshold conditions when agreeing an application by the firm to vary permission, or when varying or imposing requirements on a firm.

The FCA and the PRA will have the power to create '**threshold condition codes**'. These will elaborate on the conditions and how they will apply to different categories of firm.

4.7.2 General conditions

The following threshold conditions apply under the FCA/PRA structure.

- The applicant must have the **legal status** to carry on certain regulated activities, ie the legal structure of the business.

- Another condition considers the **location of the offices** of the applicant. If the applicant is a UK company, its head and registered offices must be located in the UK. For an applicant that is not a company, if it has its head office in the UK, then it must carry on business in the UK.

- Firms will need to ensure that no impediment to their **effective supervision** arises from: the nature and complexity of regulated activities undertaken, products offered, and the business organisation. This condition also covers the effect of **close links** of the applicant with other entities, eg other members of the same group, and whether these have an effect on effective supervision by the regulator.

- An applicant for FCA authorisation must have **appropriate resources** for the activities they seek to undertake. Such resources would not only include capital, but also non-financial resources such as personnel. Adequacy of resources will be determined by reference to the scale and nature of business, risk to the continuity of services, and the effect of a firm's membership of a group if applicable. Dual-regulated firms will need to take account of the operational objectives of the FCA and of the skills and experience of the firm's management.

- Another threshold condition relates to the **suitability** of the applicant. The firm must be considered to be 'fit and proper', ie it must have integrity, be competent and have appropriate procedures in place to comply with regulations. Suitability to carry on one regulated activity does not mean that the applicant is suitable to carry on all regulated activities. FCA-authorised firms must ensure that their affairs are conducted in an appropriate manner with regard to the interest of consumers and the integrity of the UK financial system. Those responsible for managing the affairs of a firm are to act with probity, in order to satisfy the regulators that the firm is fit and proper – in making their assessments, the regulators will consider the entirety of a firm's board and non-board senior management. Management will be required to minimise the extent to which their business could be used for financial crime.

The FCA will refuse applications at an earlier stage if it does not think that the proposed offering of products or services is in the interests of consumers or, more broadly, if it poses a significant risk to regulatory objectives.

4.7.3 FCA's Business Model Threshold Condition

The FCA will apply the **Business Model Threshold Condition**, which refers to the risk that might be posed for a firm, for its customers and for the integrity of the UK financial system.

The FCA has stated that this new threshold condition demonstrates the importance that the FCA will place on a firm's ability to put forward an appropriate, viable and sustainable business model, given the nature and scale of business it intends to carry out. The regulator will expect firms to demonstrate adequate contingency planning in their business models. Firms will be expected to make clear how their business model meets the needs of clients and customers, not placing them at undue risk, or placing at risk the integrity of the wider UK financial services industry.

4.7.4 PRA's Business to be Conducted in a Prudent Manner Threshold Condition

The PRA's **Business to be Conducted in a Prudent Manner Threshold Condition** is closely equivalent to the FCA's appropriate resources and business model conditions, which we have described above. PRA-authorised firms must hold appropriate financial and non-financial resources. Appropriate resources are evaluated by reference to complexity of activities, the liabilities of the firm, effective management, and the ability to reduce risks to the safety and soundness of the firm.

4.8 Application procedure

As we have already seen, if a firm wishes to undertake a regulated activity by way of business in the UK, it must be authorised or exempt. Earlier, we considered the scope of the exemptions (eg appointed representatives and RIE/RCHs).

A firm wishing to obtain permission (**Part 4A permission**) from the regulator to perform a regulated activity will be sent an application pack requiring detailed information from the firm and the payment of a fee. The amount of detailed information that the applicant will have to submit will be related to the risks posed to the active elements of the four regulatory objectives.

The regulator will view the application in accordance with the regulatory objectives and must be proportional in the information it requires, having regard to the nature of the applicant's business. Therefore, although some applicants will have to complete all sections of the pack, other sections are specific to certain types of business. The regulator has **six months** to determine an authorisation from the date of receipt.

The **information** an applicant must provide includes the following.

- A UK address for the service of documents
- General information about the applicant, intended activities, proposed/current unregulated activities
- How the firm will comply with the regulatory requirements
- Business plan
- Financial budget and projections

- Details of systems to be used including compliance systems
- Details of individuals managing the business, including details of any outsourcing of functions
- For insurance activities, details of the risks being underwritten

The relevant regulator will determine whether the threshold conditions have been met including whether the applicant is ready, willing and organised to comply with the regulatory obligations that will apply if it is given permission to conduct those regulated activities. The regulator may, in addition to the information provided, carry out any further enquiries about the applicant, including requiring the applicant to attend meetings to give further information, requiring information supplied to be verified (eg by an auditor or accountant) and visiting the applicant's premises. In addition, the regulator may have regard to any person who is connected to the applicant.

Connected persons would include:

- Someone who **controls** the applicant (ie owns 20% or more of the shares or who is able to exercise a significant influence over the firm's management). The regulator will determine whether that person is fit and proper to exert such influence.
- The **directors and partners** of the applicant. Where they are to be approved persons, this would include whether they are fit and proper to be approved for the controlled functions they will be exercising.
- Any **company** in the same group as the applicant.
- Any person with whom the applicant will enter into a material **outsourcing** agreement.
- Any person who may **exert influence** on the applicant, which might pose a risk to the applicant satisfying the threshold conditions.

If the application is successful, permission is granted and the direct consequence is that the applicant is authorised to carry out those activities. The firm will receive a written notice of the decision and the regulator's register of authorised persons is updated.

The regulator may, however, consider that the permissions applied for need to be modified based on the regulator's review of the applicant. They will recommend the application be granted subject to limitations or requirements or to a narrower scope of activities than the applicant originally requested. If the applicant does not accept these limitations or if the regulator simply decide to refuse the application in its entirety then the case is passed to the **Regulatory Decisions Committee (RDC)** for review. The process may result in a final reference to the Tribunal if the RDC's decision is not agreed by the applicant.

4.9 Supervision

> **Learning objective**
>
> **Know** the supervisory process: purpose of supervision arrangements; focus on a firm's senior management; risk-based approach to regulation; tools for supervision

4.9.1 Introduction

The FCA supervises the conduct of both FCA-regulated and dual-regulated firms, and also has the task of prudential regulation of FCA-regulated firms. The PRA is responsible for prudential regulation of dual-regulated firms.

4.9.2 Supervisory tools

The supervisory tools available to the regulators are of four types:

- **Diagnostic** – designed to identify, assess and measure risk
- **Monitoring** – to track the development of risks
- **Preventative** – to reduce or limit identified risks and prevent risks from crystallising
- **Remedial** – to address risks that have crystallised

In the supervisory process, the regulators may use a broad range of **tools**, including the following.

- Desk-based reviews
- Liaison with other agencies or regulators
- Meetings with the management and representatives of the firm
- On-site inspections
- Reviews and analysis of periodic returns and notifications
- Reviews of past business
- Transaction monitoring
- Use of auditors
- Use of skilled persons reports*

* Under s166 FSMA 2000, the regulator can require a firm to appoint an independent skilled person who will review a specified aspect of the business of the firm.

4.9.3 The FCA's risk assessment process

The FCA is a risk-based regulator and has declared that its risk framework will be the 'engine room' of the business, providing support to the key activities, namely: supervision, policy, enforcement and authorisation.

- Given its broad remit, the FCA will need to consider **detriment** when carrying out its risk assessments.
- In quantifying detriment, the FCA will assess **probability** and **impact**.
- Impact will be further broken down into **incidence** (for example, the number of consumers affected or potentially affected) and **severity** (for example, the amount of welfare or detriment involved per consumer).

Such assessments will be based on current understanding of the risk or opportunity as well as reasonable expectations of how they will develop under a variety of scenarios. This type of analysis will help to support the FCA's aim of intervening earlier and more swiftly to prevent detriment, by evaluating the costs and benefits of the timing of any action.

4.9.4 The FCA's approach to supervision

The statutory objectives of the FCA will drive what the organisation will do.

As we have seen, the FCA's single **strategic objective** is, in summary, **'Making markets work well'**. The FCA's three operational objectives are: ensuring consumer protection, market integrity, and competition in the interests of consumers. Of these, the newest for the FCA is the latter. As a primary statutory objective, we will be obliged to consider the role of competition (or lack of it) as a driver of poor outcomes in markets and work out how to address these problems.

The starting point for the FCA's supervision process will be the **categorisation of firms** into four new categories – C1, C2, C3 or C4 – according to their impact on consumers and the market, while recognising that there is not a one-size-fits-all approach. So, for example, C1 firms are those likely to be the largest, most complex firms with very large client assets or trading bases, whereas C4 firms are likely to be those smaller firms with simpler business models and products.

Overall, the new categorisation means that the FCA will have supervisors allocated to firms with the greatest potential to cause risks to consumers or market integrity. Given limited resources, **supervisors will be deployed flexibly to deal with problems** that arise and specific issues and products that have potential to or are already causing consumer harm.

Alongside this approach is the way in which firms will be supervised on a day-to-day basis. The **FCA supervision model** will be based on three key pillars – **FSF**, **Event Driven**, and **Issues & Products**.

The FCA's forward-looking assessment of a firm's conduct risks will be undertaken within a new **Firm Systematic Framework (FSF).** This is designed to answer the key question of 'Are the interests of customers and market integrity at the heart of how the firm is run?'

The FSF will involve:

- Analysing firms' business models and strategies so that the FCA can form a view of the sustainability of the business from a conduct perspective and where future risks might lie, and

- Assessment of how the fair treatment of customers and ensuring market integrity is embedded in the way in which the firm runs its business, from the 'tone from the top', through how culture is embedded across the firm, to how the firm manages and controls its risks.

The approach will be differentiated depending on the categorisation of the firm. Broadly, C1 and C2 firms will experience the most intensive focus and shorter, two-year regulatory cycles. C3 and C4 firms will too have their business models evaluated, but this will be done on a four-year cycle and through a combination of risk profiling, which will determine which firms will be interviewed.

The **second pillar** is based on dealing with **issues that are emerging** or have happened and are unforeseen in their nature. This is termed '**event-driven work**' and will cover matters from mergers and acquisitions, to whistleblowing allegations, to spikes in reported complaints at a firm. The FCA will seek to secure customer redress, where applicable.

The **final pillar** is broadly termed '**issues and products**' and will be largely driven by the analysis made of each sector by the regulator's sector teams. These teams will produce Sector Risk Assessments of conduct risks across all sectors. This will determine whether there are cross-firm and/or product issues driving poor outcomes for consumers or endangering market integrity, the degree of potential detriment, and whether the regulator should be undertaking any thematic pieces of work to assess or mitigate these risks.

The FCA will adopt a differentiated approach depending on how it prudentially categorises a firm. Firms will, in addition to the C1 to C4 categorisation, also be allocated one of three **prudential categories**. **CP1** firms are those whose failure would have a significant impact on the market in which they operate, but where the FCA is not yet confident that orderly wind-down can be achieved. These will still be supervised on a going-concern basis with the aim of minimising the probability of failure. Firms that have a significant market impact but for which an orderly wind-down can be achieved, will be categorised as **CP2** and supervised on a proactive 'gone-concern' basis.

Those where failure, even if disorderly, is unlikely to have significant impact, will be categorised as **CP3** and supervised on a reactive gone-concern basis.

For the vast majority of firms, the focus will be on managing failure when it happens, rather than focusing on reducing its probability.

4.9.5 The PRA's approach to supervision

The PRA proposes to adopt a 'judgement-based', forward-looking approach to supervision. Various **supervisory tools** will be available to the regulator, including: analysis of public information or that provided by firms, meetings with firms, inspections, on-site testing and stress testing, liaison with firms' external auditors, and liaison with the FCA. The level of core supervisory activity the PRA will carry out with a firm will depend on the firm's category. The Authority will have discretion to carry out additional work beyond the core on areas of particular concern.

The PRA plans to classify the firms it supervises into five categories, from high impact (1) to low impact (5), based on their potential impact on the stability of the UK's financial system.

- Firms that are most significant, given their size, complexity, interconnectedness and business type, have the capacity to cause 'very significant disruption' to the UK financial system, and so are categorised as '**high impact**'.
- **Low impact** firms have no significant capacity on their own to cause disruption, even though there is the potential that they could contribute to disruption that is occurring across a sector of the financial system.

The PRA will take into account **how close a firm is to failing** when considering the actions it will take. The PRA's '**Proactive Intervention Framework (PIF)**' will characterise the PRA's judgement about a firm's **proximity to failure**.

The PIF is designed to ensure that the PRA puts into effect its aim to identify and respond to emerging risks at an early stage. There will be five clearly demarcated PIF stages, each denoting a different proximity to failure, and every firm will sit in a particular stage at each point in time.

The five stages of the PIF

- Stage 1 – Low risk to viability of firm
- Stage 2 – Moderate risk to viability of firm
- Stage 3 – Risk to viability absent action by the firm
- Stage 4 – Imminent risk to viability of firm
- Stage 5 – Firm in resolution or being actively wound up

As a firm moves to a higher PIF stage – that is, as the PRA judges that the firm's viability has deteriorated – the senior management of firms will be expected to ensure they take appropriate remedial action to reduce the likelihood of failure, and the authorities will ensure appropriate preparedness for resolution.

For example, at Stage 3, a firm may be formally required to draw on the menu of options set out in its recovery plan.

4.10 Transaction reporting

Learning objective: Know the transaction reporting regime

The regulator's **Transaction Monitoring Unit** is responsible for surveillance of UK markets, for the collection of transaction reports from the industry and for monitoring firms' compliance with the **transaction reporting rules**. These rules on reporting transactions apply under MiFID.

Firms entering into reportable transactions must transmit to the regulator reports containing the mandatory details for those transactions. These are collected through the **ZEN** surveillance system, which went live in August 2011, superseding the previous Sabre II system.

2: THE FINANCIAL SERVICES AND MARKETS ACT 2000

Reportable transactions

- Transactions in financial instruments listed on a regulated market or prescribed market
- Transactions in over the counter (OTC) derivatives based on single equity- or debt-related financial instruments listed on regulated or prescribed markets (not index derivatives such as those based on the FTSE 100 index)

Reportable information includes the identity of the ultimate client in a transaction, or of the identity of the firm dealing with the ultimate client.

Reportable information

- Reporting firm
- Trading date and time
- Buy or Sell (from perspective of reporting firm, or client)
- Trading capacity (eg, as principal or agent, or agency cross where firm acts as agent for both buying and selling counterparties)
- Instrument identification (ISIN code, where applicable), or description and type (for OTC derivatives)
- Underlying instrument, derivative type, maturity date and strike price (for OTC derivatives)
- Put or Call (for OTC derivatives)
- Unit price and currency code (and price multiplier – number of underlying instruments represented – for OTC derivatives)
- Quantity (volume) of transaction
- Counterparty and customer/client identification code
- Venue (market) identification
- Firm's unique transaction identification number

Branches of EEA firms providing a service in the UK are required to report their UK transactions to the regulator. To avoid the burden of having to report to two different national regulators, such branches may choose to report their non-UK as well as their UK transactions to the UK (host State) regulator only.

Firms need not report transactions that are already covered by other approved reporting mechanisms, such as those of regulated markets (eg, the LSE) and multilateral trading facilities (MTFs). Thus, a firm providing discretionary portfolio management services and using an external broker may usually rely on the fact that the broker is required to report transactions and need not itself report the transactions to the regulator.

Transactions in commodity, interest rate and foreign exchange derivatives are not reportable.

The transaction information collected is used for the following **purposes**.

- Monitoring for market abuse (insider trading) and market manipulation
- Firm supervision – to help identify breaches of conduct of business rules etc
- Market supervision – to alert the regulator to potential new risks to market confidence, eg growth in use of certain financial instruments
- Exchange of transaction reports with other EEA competent authorities through the Committee of European Securities Regulators (CESR)
- Use of transaction reports by certain external parties, including the Bank of England and the Takeover Panel

4.11 Approval process

> **Learning objective**
>
> **Know** the approval processes for Approved Persons: the application process; the criteria for approval as an Approved Person

Certain **individuals** within an authorised firm will require **approval** from the regulators because they carry out **controlled functions**. We explain what the controlled functions are below.

It is important to appreciate that the process of an **individual** obtaining **approved person** status is different from the process of a **firm** obtaining **authorisation**.

To obtain approval, a person must satisfy the regulator that they are **fit and proper** to carry out the controlled function. The suitability of a member of staff who performs a controlled function is covered in the **Fit and Proper Test for Approved Persons** (part of the High Level Standards section of the regulatory Handbook).

The most important considerations are the following.

- **Honesty, integrity and reputation**. The relevant regulator will examine whether the person's reputation might have an adverse impact on the firm they are performing a controlled function for. This will include looking at a number of factors including any criminal convictions, civil claims, previous disciplinary proceedings, censure or investigations by any regulator, exchange, governing body or court; any other previous contraventions of regulations; any complaints which have been upheld; connections with any body which has previously been refused a registration, authorisation or licence or had such registrations, authorisations or licences revoked or been expelled by a regulatory or governmental body; whether they have had any management role within any entities which have gone into liquidation; whether they have been dismissed or asked to resign from a similar position or position of trust; disqualifications as a director, and finally whether they have been candid and truthful in their dealings with regulatory bodies and demonstrated a willingness to comply with regulatory and legal standards. When looking at previous convictions, even old (ie spent) convictions, as defined in the Rehabilitation of Offenders Act 1974, can be taken into account.

- **Competence and capability**. The regulator will examine whether the Training and Competence requirements have been complied with or whether the person has demonstrated by training and experience that they are suitable to perform the controlled function. If a person has been convicted, or dismissed or suspended from employment due to drug or alcohol abuse this will be considered in relation only to their continuing ability to perform that function. In addition, s61 FSMA 2000 emphasises that the fit and proper test for approved persons includes assessing qualifications, training and competence. It is not a requirement that a person has experience in order to be approved.

- **Financial soundness**. The regulator will consider whether the applicant has any outstanding judgement debts, has filed for bankruptcy or been involved in any similar proceedings. The fact that a person is of limited financial resources will not, in itself, affect their suitability to perform a controlled function.

These criteria must be met on a continuing basis. Individuals performing a controlled function must obtain approval **before** they take up the role. Approved persons must adhere to the seven **Statements of Principle**, which were discussed earlier.

It is the obligation of the authorised firm for which the person works to apply to the relevant regulator for approval for each controlled function to be undertaken.

2: THE FINANCIAL SERVICES AND MARKETS ACT 2000

FSMA 2000 allows the regulator **three months** from the time it receives a properly completed application to come to a decision, although most straightforward applications are dealt with in a matter of a few days. Approved persons applications must be completed through the **Online Notifications and Applications (ONA)** system. (This online system replaced the previous paper-based application process in October 2010.)

Where a person ceases to perform a controlled function, the firm must notify the regulator **within seven business days**. However, where a firm is effecting a 'dirty withdrawal', eg where an employee has been dismissed or there are concerns relating to their fitness and propriety, this information should be passed to the regulator immediately.

Where approval is given, the regulator's register of approved persons will be updated. Where the regulator wishes to reject an application for approval, this is referred to the **Regulatory Decisions Committee (RDC)** and may be further referred to the Tribunal where agreement is not reached.

4.12 Controlled functions

> **Learning objective**
> Understand the FCA's and PRA's controlled functions: the five functional areas, the required functions, the four areas of significant influence functions, the requirement for FCA and PRA approval prior to performing the function

Section 59 FSMA 2000 and the **Supervision Manual (SUP)** states that a person cannot carry out a controlled function in a firm unless that individual has been **approved** by the relevant regulator.

Note that we are now referring to the individual members of staff of an authorised firm. When a person is performing a controlled function and is not approved, there is a breach of statutory duty and a private person has the right to sue their firm for damages if they have suffered loss, using s71 FSMA 2000.

The **FCA** may specify a function as a **controlled function** if the individual performing it is:

- Exerting a significant influence on the conduct of the firm's affairs
- Dealing directly with customers, or
- Dealing with the property of customers

The **PRA** may specify a function as a **controlled function** if, in relation to carrying on a regulated activity by a PRA-authorised firm, it is a 'significant-influence' function.

The specific controlled functions are split into groups as shown in the following Table. (The numbering is discontinuous because of past re-categorisations of functions.)

As shown in the Table, there are:

- FCA-controlled functions for FCA-authorised firms (**FCAcont FCAauth** in the Table)
- FCA-controlled functions for PRA-authorised firms (**FCAcont PRAauth**), and
- PRA-controlled functions for PRA-authorised firms (**PRAcont PRAauth**)

Group	Function (CF)	FCAcont FCAauth	FCAcont PRAauth	PRAcont PRAauth
Governing functions	1. Director	•	•	
	2 (PRA). PRA firm Non-executive Director		•	•
	2 (FCA). FCA firm Non-executive Director	•		
	3. Chief executive	•	•	•
	4. Partner	•	•	
	5. Director of unincorporated association	•	•	
	6. Small Friendly Society	•	•	

2: THE FINANCIAL SERVICES AND MARKETS ACT 2000

Group	Function (CF)	FCAcont FCAauth	FCAcont PRAauth	PRAcont PRAauth
Required functions	8. Apportionment and oversight	•	•	
	10. Compliance oversight	•	•	
	10a. CASS operational oversight	•	•	
	11. Money laundering reporting	•	•	
	12. Actuarial			•
	12A. With-profits actuary			•
	12B. Lloyd's actuary			•
Systems and controls function	28. Systems and controls	•		•
Significant management function	29. Significant management	•	•	
Customer functions	30. Customer function	•	•	

The overall scope of the approved persons regime is not changed with the changeover from the FSA to the FCA and PRA. However, future changes are anticipated following consultations, including a **proposed CF31 function for mortgage advisers**.

Individuals who fall within all of the above categories **except** customer functions would be considered to be exerting a **significant influence** on the conduct of the firm's affairs. The previous regulator (the FSA) strengthened its approach to 'significant influence' functions (**SIFs**) by ensuring that those likely to exert a significant influence on a firm fall within the scope of the approved persons regime. The regulators will place greater emphasis on the role of senior management, including non-executive directors (NEDs). The regulators consider that it is important that directors and senior managers at firms understand their regulatory obligations and have the relevant competencies and experience to carry out their roles with integrity.

In adopting a **more 'intrusive' approach**, the regulators will focus more on the **competence and capability** of candidates for **SIFs**. For example, the previous regulator (the FSA) has carried out interviews for 'significant influence' posts at high impact firms. Once in post, where individuals fail to meet the required standards, the regulator will consider enforcement action.

Note the following points about particular functions.

- **Governing functions**. A firm will have one or more approved persons responsible (eg the Board of Directors) for directing its affairs.

- **Required functions: Apportionment and oversight function**. A director or senior manager will be responsible for either or both of the functions of apportionment of responsibilities, and oversight of systems and controls.

- **Systems and controls function**. This is the function of acting in the capacity of an employee of the firm with responsibility for reporting to the governing body of a firm, or the audit committee (or its equivalent) in relation to (1) its financial affairs, (2) setting and controlling its risk exposure, and (3) adherence to internal systems and controls, procedures and policies.

- **Significant management function**. It is expected that only a few firms will need to seek approval for an individual to perform this function. In most firms, those approved for the governing functions, required functions and the systems and controls function are likely to exercise all the significant influence at senior management level.

- **Customer function**. This applies to activities carried on from a UK establishment and has to do with giving advice on, dealing and arranging deals in and managing investments. (It does not apply to banking business such as deposit-taking and lending.)

4.13 Training and Competence regime

Learning objective

Know the Training and Competence regime: the application of the systems and control responsibilities in relation to the competence of employees; assessing and maintaining competence, the examination requirements before starting activities, how firms must assess at the outset and at regular intervals the training needs of their employees, maintaining competence; activities to which the T&C rules apply

4.13.1 Overview

Principle 3 of the **Principles for Businesses** requires firms to take reasonable care to organise and control its affairs responsibly and effectively, with adequate risk management systems. This implies having appropriate systems of control, including ensuring that **employees maintain and enhance competence**.

SYSC states that a firm's systems and controls should enable it to satisfy itself of the suitability of anyone who acts for it. A requirement under **MiFID** is that firms must employ personnel with the skills, knowledge and expertise necessary for the discharge of the responsibilities allocated to them.

The **Training and Competence (TC)** sourcebook within the FCA Handbook applies only to firms whose employees advise **retail clients, customers or consumers**.

The TC Sourcebook does not apply to firms 'passported-in' from other EEA countries.

Appropriate examination requirements no longer apply to **wholesale business** in the financial services sector.

4.13.2 The competent employees rule

Competence means having the skills, knowledge and expertise needed to discharge the responsibilities of an employee's role. This includes achieving a good standard of **ethical behaviour**.

- The **competent employees rule** is now the main Handbook requirement relating to the competence of employees. The purpose of the TC Sourcebook is to support the regulator's supervisory function by supplementing the competent employees rule for **retail activities**.

- The **competent employees rule** is that firms must employ personnel with the skills, knowledge and expertise necessary for the discharge of the responsibilities allocated to them. This rule applies to non-MiFID firms as well as **MiFID** firms.

4.13.3 Assessment of competence and supervision

A firm must not assess an employee as competent to carry on an activity until the employee has demonstrated the necessary competence to do so and passed each module of an **appropriate examination**, where required. This assessment need not take place before the employee starts to carry on the activity. However, if the employee carries on the activity, the firm must ensure that the employee gains an appropriate qualification **within 30 months** of starting to carry on that activity.

- If the adviser does not complete the qualification within 30 months, they must stop carrying out the activity until they have passed.

- This rule started on 1 January 2011 and so the earliest that this will apply to anyone is 30 June 2013.

- In calculating the 30 months, periods of time spent on the activity during different periods of employment are aggregated, and periods of 60 business days or more of an employee's continuous absence from work are excluded.

For advisers within scope of the **RDR**, there are different deadlines for those who were assessed as competent at an earlier date – ie, before 1 January 2011 (see later in this Section).

A firm must not allow an employee to carry on an activity without appropriate **supervision**.

A firm must ensure that an employee –such as a trainee adviser – does not carry on an activity (other than an overseeing activity) for which there is an examination requirement without first passing the relevant **regulatory module** of an appropriate examination.

4.13.4 Ongoing assessment

Firms should ensure that their employees' training needs are assessed at the outset and at regular intervals (including if their role changes). Appropriate training and support should be provided to ensure that training needs are satisfied. The quality and effectiveness of such training should be reviewed regularly.

Firms must review regularly and frequently employees' competence and take appropriate action to ensure that they remain competent for their role.

An employee is, of course, additionally subject to the **fit and proper test** on becoming an **approved person**.

A firm should ensure that employees **maintain their competence**, for example through a formal programme of **Continuing Professional Development (CPD)**.

4.13.5 Appropriate examination requirements

Under the '**RDR Professionalism**' rules, appropriate examination requirements apply to firms advising **retail clients** on **retail investment products (RIPs)**, whether advisers are engaged in providing **independent advice** or **restricted advice**.

Requirements to hold an 'appropriate qualification' apply to individuals carrying out one or more of the following regulated activities for **retail clients**:

- Advising on (but not dealing in) securities (which are not stakeholder pension schemes or broker funds)
- Advising on (but not dealing in) derivatives
- Advising on retail investment products (which are not broker funds)
- Advising on Friendly Society tax-exempt policies
- Advising on, and dealing in securities (which are not stakeholder pension schemes or broker funds)
- Advising on and dealing with or for clients in derivatives

There is not a qualification requirement for:

- 'Basic' (scripted) advice on stakeholder products
- Advice on friendly society life policies where the employee's annual remuneration from them will not exceed £1,000
- Advice on non-investment insurance contracts

If an individual performs any of the RDR TC activities and so acts as a retail investment adviser – even if this is only on one occasion – then they will still need an **appropriate RDR qualification** and need to be approved to carry out the controlled function: **CF30 Customer Function**.

Appropriate Qualification Tables in the regulator's **Training and Competence Sourcebook** (TC, Appendix 4E) detail which are the appropriate qualifications for the various activities requiring qualifications.

Under the RDR qualifications rules, there are two important deadlines for those who were previously assessed as competent:

- Advisers who were deemed competent on or before 30 June 2009 must have attained an **appropriate RDR-compliant qualification** by the **end of 2012** – the first **RDR qualification deadline**.

- For advisers who are assessed as competent between 1 July 2009 and 1 January 2011, the **second RDR deadline** of **1 July 2013** applies for obtaining their RDR qualification.

- Those who **started giving advice** on or after 1 January 2011 will have a rolling qualification deadline of 30 months from the date they begin the activity.

Advisers already holding certain appropriate qualifications do not need to take further exams to meet RDR standards, but are likely to need to carry out qualifications **gap-fill** using relevant structured **continuing professional development (CPD)**.

Some advisers may choose to reach the required standards (eg, if they do not want to take the exam route) by undertaking an alternative assessment available from some providers.

4.13.6 Specialist examinations

Specialist examinations must be completed in addition for giving advice in the areas shown below. (Activity numbers are as listed in TC Appendix 1.)

Pensions transfer / opt-out specialists and broker fund advisers must attain the specialist examinations before acting in those roles. For other specialist roles listed below, advisers must be monitored by a competent person until an appropriate exam is passed.

- Regulated mortgage contracts advice (Activity number 20)
- Equity release (Activity number 21)
- Long-term care insurance contracts (Activity number 7)
- Pension transfer and specialist (Activity number 11)
- Broker fund adviser (Activity number 10)

4.13.7 Notification requirements for firms

As part of the regulator's new **risk-based supervisory strategy for individuals,** since **July 2011** firms have been required to notify the regulator of adviser competence issues.

A firm must notify the FCA as soon as they become aware, or have information that suggests any of the following has occurred, or **may have** occurred, in relation to any of its advisers:

- An adviser who has been assessed as competent is no longer considered competent

- An adviser has failed to attain an appropriate qualification within the prescribed time limit

- An adviser has failed to comply with a Statement of Principle in carrying out his/her controlled function

- An adviser has performed an activity to which the training and competence (TC) requirements apply before having demonstrated the necessary competence and without appropriate supervision

Why does the regulator need this information? The information gathered will be fed, along with data from other sources, into an adviser database that has the objective of identifying the highest risk advisers.

4.13.8 Maintaining competence

Continuing Professional Development (CPD) is a term used to describe the process an individual needs to go through to keep their knowledge and skills up to date.

The FCA Handbook (TC2.1.13G) states that a firm should ensure that **maintaining competence** for an employee takes into account such matters as:

- Technical knowledge and its application
- Skills and expertise
- Changes in the market and to products, legislation and regulation

These aspects may vary, for example according to whether an individual is independent or tied, is a general financial planner or specialist, or whether they have any managerial responsibilities within the firm. For example, a supervisor attending a coaching course could reasonably use this as CPD – it is not restricted just to technical knowledge.

Firms should have systems in place to be able to monitor an individual's competence. This is likely to focus on either the activities undertaken to maintain competence, eg **CPD records**, or **tests** used to ensure that knowledge is acceptable at any point. In practice, both methods are likely to be used.

4.13.9 T&C record-keeping

A firm must make appropriate records to demonstrate compliance with the rules in TC and keep them for the following periods after an employee stops carrying on the activity:

- At least five years for MiFID business
- Three years for non-MiFID business, and
- Indefinitely for a pension transfer specialist

4.14 Whistleblowing

> **Learning objective**
>
> **Know** the legal and regulatory basis for whistleblowing

Part of the regulatory Handbook relating to Senior Management Arrangements, Systems and Controls covers procedures relating to '**whistleblowing**'.

The regulatory rules and guidance serve to:

- Remind firms that there is legislation covering whistleblowing which applies to authorised firms (**Public Interest Disclosure Act 1998**, '**PIDA**')
- Encourage firms to adopt and communicate procedures for employees to raise concerns about the risk management arrangements of the firm

Whistleblowing is the process whereby a worker seeks to make a **protected disclosure** to a regulator or law enforcement agency outside the firm, in good faith, of information which tends to show that one or more of the following activities is, or is likely, to be committed or is being deliberately concealed by their employer.

- A criminal offence
- A failure to comply with a legal obligation
- A miscarriage of justice
- A breach of health and safety rules
- Damage to the environment

A firm cannot include a clause in the employee's contract preventing the employee from making such a disclosure, ie from 'blowing the whistle' on their employer's practices. The rules apply even if the activity listed above occurs outside the UK.

In addition, if the firm or member of staff of an authorised firm were to discriminate against an employee who made a disclosure in any way, the regulator would regard this as a serious matter. In particular the regulator would question the firm's '**suitability**' under the **Threshold Conditions** and the individual's **fitness and propriety**. In serious cases, the regulator can withdraw the firm's authorisation and an individual's approval.

Chapter Roundup

- No firm may carry on a regulated activity, unless either authorised, or exempt from authorisation. Some activities (eg media coverage, but not tipsheets) are excluded from the authorisation requirement. No individual may carry on a controlled function unless they are an approved person.

- Dual-regulated firms (banks and building societies, credit unions, insurers and some investment firms) are authorised by the PRA but only with FCA approval. FCA-only regulated firms (including independent financial advisers, investment exchanges, insurance brokers and fund managers) are authorised by the FCA.

- Regulatory enforcement measures include public censure, unlimited fines, restitution orders and cancellation of authorisation or approval. Various Statutory Notices may be issued in cases involving the FCA's Regulatory Decisions Committee.

- The Tax and Chancery Chamber of the Upper Tribunal (TCCUT) can re-hear enforcement and authorisation cases.

- The regulators have wide powers to visit firms' premises without notice and to require documents to be produced.

- The Regulated Activities Order specifies the list of regulated activities, and the specified investments covered by FSMA 2000.

- A firm may be authorised through obtaining 'Part 4A permission' or, for EEA firms, through passporting. The relevant regulator's threshold conditions must be met for authorisation, which are specific to the types of activities the firm carries out.

- The regulators' approach to supervision is 'risk-based', so that supervisory effort is directed at higher risk areas.

- In accordance with MiFID, all equity and debt-related transactions must be reported to the regulator, who collects the transaction reports through the ZEN surveillance system.

- Those carrying out a controlled function need to meet a 'fit and proper' test to be approved persons. This test covers honesty, integrity and reputation; competence and capability; and financial soundness.

- Controlled functions include exerting significant influence on the firm, and dealing with customers or their property.

- A firm is responsible for ensuring that there is appropriate training for employees and that employees remain competent. There are appropriate examination requirements for those carrying out specified regulated activities with retail clients.

- A 'whistleblowing' employee can make a protected disclosure to a regulator or law enforcement agency of wrongdoing.

2: THE FINANCIAL SERVICES AND MARKETS ACT 2000

Test Your Knowledge

Check your knowledge of the chapter here, without referring back to the text.

1.	What is s19 FSMA? What does it require?	
2.	What are the penalties for breaching the general prohibition?	
3.	Can you name three types of exempt persons?	▪ ▪ ▪
4.	What is the RDC and what is its role?	
5.	Can you name three excluded activities?	▪ ▪ ▪
6.	Can you name four threshold conditions?	▪ ▪ ▪ ▪
7.	'The ZEN surveillance system processes data on all UK equity transactions, even those on which the regulator has no grounds for suspicion.' True, or False?	

8.	What is the difference between authorisation and approval?	
9.	What legislation covers 'whistleblowing'?	

2: THE FINANCIAL SERVICES AND MARKETS ACT 2000

Test Your Knowledge: Answers

1. Section 19 FSMA 2000 is called the 'general prohibition'. It requires a company to be authorised if it is carrying out regulated activities by way of business in the UK (unless it is exempt or excluded).

   (See Section 1.1)

2. Penalties for breach of s19 FSMA 2000 include criminal and civil sanctions. The maximum criminal penalty is two years in prison and/or an unlimited fine (in the Crown Court). Civil penalties include contracts being unenforceable, compensation, injunctions and restitution orders.

   (See Section 1.2)

3. You could have mentioned any three of the following (mnemonic: **April**): **A**ppointed Representatives, **P**rofessional people, **RI**Es, **RO**IEs, **RC**Hs, **I**nstitutions, eg the Bank of England and **L**loyd's members.

   (See Section 1.7)

4. The RDC is the Regulatory Decisions Committee. The RDC is outside the FCA's management structure and is used to decide on action in enforcement cases and also on withdrawing, varying or refusing authorisation or approval.

   (See Section 2.1)

5. Recall the word **Demote**: **D**ealing as principal where the person is not holding themselves out to the market as willing to deal, **E**mployee share schemes, **M**edia, **O**verseas persons, **T**rustees, nomin**E**es and personal representatives. You could have mentioned any three.

   (See Section 4.3)

6. You could have mentioned any four of: legal status, location of offices, effective supervision, appropriate resources, suitability, business model (FCA), and business to be conducted in a prudent manner (PRA).

   (See Section 4.7)

7. True. Data is collected by the regulator on all transactions in equities on regulated or prescribed markets.

   (See Section 4.10)

8. A firm needs to be authorised under s19 FSMA 2000 if it is carrying out regulated activities by way of business in the UK. An individual requires approval under s59 FSMA 2000 if he/she is undertaking one of the controlled functions, eg as director, or compliance oversight.

   (See Sections 1.6, 4.11 – 4.12)

9. The Public Interest Disclosure Act 1998 (PIDA).

   (See Section 4.14)

3

Associated Legislation and Regulation

INTRODUCTION

There are various measures designed to deal with crimes relating to the financial services sector. It is important to know the law so that one does not inadvertently breach it, as ignorance of the law is not a defence.

The UK regulator has made substantial revisions to its rules to comply with the Markets in Financial Instruments Directive (MiFID). To a substantial degree, this has been achieved by 'copying out' MiFID provisions.

We also look in this chapter at the provisions relating to other European Directives, data protection and the capital adequacy of investment firms.

CHAPTER CONTENTS

	Page
1 Insider Dealing	77
2 Market Abuse and Manipulation	80
3 Money Laundering	85
4 Terrorism	98
5 Disclosure and Transparency	101
6 Data Protection and Record-Keeping	103
7 Prudential Standards	105
8 Regulation Through European Directives	109
Chapter Roundup	114
Test Your Knowledge	115

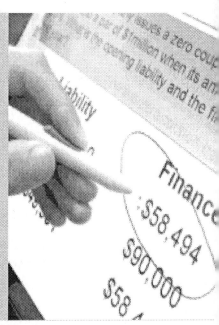

3: ASSOCIATED LEGISLATION AND REGULATION

Learning Objectives

Insider dealing

- **Understand** the meaning of 'inside information' and 'insider', the offences and the instruments covered by the legislation
- **Know** the general defences available with regard to insider dealing
- **Know** the special defences: market makers acting in good faith, market information and price stabilisation
- **Know** the FCA's powers to prosecute insider dealing

Market abuse

- **Understand** the statutory offence of market abuse
- **Know** the status of FCA's Code of Market Conduct; the territorial scope of the legislation and regulation
- **Know** the offences outlined in the Code of Market Conduct
- **Know** the concept of effect rather than intention; the concept of a reasonable regular user and accepted market practices
- **Understand** the enforcement regime for market abuse and a firm's duty to report suspicious transactions
- **Know** the statutory exceptions (safe harbours) to market abuse

Money laundering

- **Understand** the terms 'money laundering', 'criminal conduct' and 'criminal property' and the application of money laundering to all crimes and the power of the Secretary of State to determine what is 'relevant criminal conduct'
- **Understand** that the UK legislation on money laundering is found in the Proceeds of Crime Act 2002 (POCA 2002) as amended by the Serious Organised Crime and Police Act 2005 (SOCPA 2005), the Money Laundering Regulations 2007, the Senior Management Arrangements, Systems and Controls Sourcebook (SYSC) and that guidance to these provisions is found in the Joint Money Laundering Steering Group Guidance, and **understand** the interaction between them
- **Understand** the main offence set out in the Money Laundering Regulations (internal controls), which includes obligations on firms for adequate training of individuals on money laundering
- **Understand** the three stages of money laundering
- **Understand** the main offences of assistance, ie concealing, arrangements, acquisition, use and possession; failure to disclose; tipping off in the regulated sector; and the implications of Part 7 POCA 2002 regarding the objective test in relation to reporting suspicious transactions; that appropriate disclosure (internal for staff and to the National Crime Agency for the firm) is a defence
- **Understand** the approach covered by the Senior Management Arrangements, Systems and Controls Sourcebook (SYSC), in particular, the systems and controls that the FCA and PRA expect firms to have adopted, the role of the Money Laundering Reporting Officer, Nominated Officer and the compliance function

3: ASSOCIATED LEGISLATION AND REGULATION

- **Understand** the standards expected by the 2007 JMLSG Guidance Notes particularly in relation to:
  - Risk-based approach
  - Requirements for directors and senior managers to be responsible for money laundering precautions
  - Need for risk assessment
  - Need for enhanced due diligence in relation to politically exposed persons
  - Need for high level policy statement
  - Detailed procedures implementing the firm's risk based approach
  - Financial sanctions regime

- **Understand** the Money Laundering aspects of know your customer (Joint Money Laundering Steering Groups' Guidance for the Financial Sector)

- **Understand** the importance of ongoing monitoring of business relationships and being able to recognise a suspicious transaction, and the requirement for staff to report to the MLRO and for the firm to report to the National Crime Agency

- **Know** what activities are regarded as 'terrorism' in the UK (Terrorism Act 2000 Part 1), the obligations on regulated firms under the Counter-Terrorism Act 2008 (money laundering of terrorist funds) and the Anti-Terrorism, Crime and Security Act 2001, Schedule 2, Part 3 (disclosure of information) and where to find the sanction list for terrorist activities

- **Understand** the importance of preventative measures in respect of terrorist financing and the essential differences between laundering the proceeds of crime and the financing of terrorist acts and the interaction between the rules of the FCA, the PRA, the Terrorism Act 2000 and the JMLSG Guidance regarding terrorism

Model Code

- **Know** the main purpose and provisions of the Model Code on share dealing by directors and other persons discharging managerial responsibilities including: close periods, undisclosed inside information, Chairman's approval, dealings by the Chairman, short-term dealing, exceptional circumstances, application and record keeping

Disclosure and Transparency Rules

- **Know** the purpose of the Disclosure and Transparency Rules and the control of information

Data Protection Act 1998

- **Know** the eight Data Protection principles, the need for notification of data controllers with the Information Commissioner; the record-keeping requirements of FCA-regulated firms

Relevant European regulation

- **Know** the relevant European Union Directives and the impact on the UK financial services industry in respect of:
  - Passporting within the EEA (MiFID)
  - Home v host state regulation (MiFID)
  - Selling cross-border collective investment schemes
  - Selling securities cross-border (Prospectus Directive)

Prudential Standards

- **Know** the purpose of the capital adequacy requirements
- **Know** the purpose, scope and application of the liquidity framework requirements and how they apply to regulated firms

1 INSIDER DEALING

Learning objective: Understand the offences and the instruments covered by the legislation

1.1 Introduction

Insider dealing is the offence of acting with information that is not freely and openly available to all other participants in the market place. This became an offence in 1980 but the current legislation making it a criminal offence is found in **Part V** of the **Criminal Justice Act 1993 (CJA 1993)**.

CJA 1993 makes it a **criminal offence** for connected persons who receive inside information to act on that information.

The legislation (Schedule 2) covers shares, debt securities, warrants, depository receipts, and options, futures or contracts for differences (CfDs) on any of these types of security.

1.2 Insider

Learning objective: Understand the meaning of 'inside information' and 'insider'

An insider is defined under CJA 1993 as an individual who has **information** in his possession that he **knows** is **inside information** and **knows** is from an **inside source**.

Inside information in this context refers to **unpublished price-sensitive information** that is **specific or precise** and **relates to a security or its issuer**.

What is **published** information? The following information is deemed to be 'published'.

- Information published via a regulated market, eg an RIE
- Information contained in public records
- Information which can otherwise be readily acquired by market-users, eg in the financial press
- Information derived from public information
- Information which can only be acquired by expertise or by payment of a fee
- Information which is published only to a section of the public, rather than the public in general, or published outside the UK
- Information which can be acquired by observation, eg a factory burning down

An inside source is **an individual** and would include a **director**, **employee** or **shareholder** of an issuer of securities or a person having access to the information by virtue of their employment, office or profession.

A person will also be an inside source if he receives the information directly or indirectly from one of the above and satisfies the general definition above.

1.3 Offences

If a person satisfies the definition of an insider, it is an offence for that person:

- To **deal** in the affected securities either on a regulated market or through a professional intermediary
- To **encourage another** person to deal with reasonable cause to believe that dealing would take place on a regulated market or through a professional intermediary
- To **disclose the information** to another person other than in the proper performance of their duties

1.4 General defences

> **Learning objective**
>
> **Know** the general defences available with regard to insider dealing

An individual is not guilty of insider **dealing** if he can show that:

- He did not, at the time, expect the dealing to result in a profit attributable to the fact that the information was price sensitive
- At the time, he believed on reasonable grounds that the information had been disclosed widely enough to ensure that none of those taking part in the dealing would be prejudiced by not having the information
- He would have done what he did even if he had not had the information

A similar series of defences are available to the charge of **encouraging** another to deal in price-affected securities.

An individual is not guilty of insider dealing by virtue of a **disclosure** of information if he shows that:

- He did not, at the time, expect any person, because of the disclosure, to deal in securities either through a regulated market or via a professional intermediary
- Although he had such an expectation at the time, he did not expect the dealing to result in a profit attributable to the fact that the information was price sensitive in relation to the securities

1.5 Special defences

> **Learning objective**
>
> **Know** the special defences: market makers acting in good faith, market information and price stabilisation

1.5.1 Market makers

A market maker is a person who holds himself out at all normal times in compliance with the rules of a RIE as willing to acquire or dispose of securities and is required to do so under those rules. An individual is not guilty of insider dealing by virtue of dealing in securities or encouraging another to deal if he can show that he acted in **good faith** in the course of market making.

1.5.2 Market information

An individual is not guilty of an offence under CJA 1993 if he can show that the information which he had as an insider was **market information** (information concerning transactions in securities that either have been or are about to be undertaken) and that it was reasonable for an individual in his position to have acted in that manner when in possession of inside information. Consideration will be taken as to the content of the information, the circumstances of receiving the information and the capacity in which the recipient acts, to determine whether it is reasonable.

This defence will also cover the **facilitation of takeover bids**.

1.5.3 Price stabilisation

An individual is not guilty of an offence under the Act by virtue of dealing in securities or encouraging another person to deal if he can show that he acted in conformity with the **price stabilisation rules**.

1.6 Enforcement

> **Learning objective**
>
> **Know** the FCA's powers to prosecute insider dealing

The FCA has powers (under FSMA 2000) to prosecute a range of criminal offences, including **insider dealing**, in England, Wales and Northern Ireland.

Under s168 FSMA 2000, inspectors from the FCA have the power to require persons who they believe may have information to:

- Produce any relevant documents
- Attend before them
- Give all assistance possible

In addition to prosecuting for insider dealing, the regulator may revoke the authorisation of an authorised firm where individuals have been allowed to insider deal. They can also remove a person's approval.

Amendments made in 2009 to the Serious Organised Crime and Police Act 2005 gave the regulator additional statutory powers, including the **power to grant 'immunity notices'**, when investigating criminal cases such as insider dealing.

While the Department for Business, Innovation and Skills has the power to prosecute, the **FCA** will normally prosecute insider dealing cases. Accordingly, the London Stock Exchange (as the entity who often initiates an investigation) will pass information directly to the regulator.

1.7 Penalties

Insider dealing is a **criminal offence** and the penalties available depend on the method of prosecution.

- **Magistrates' Court** – maximum of six months' imprisonment and a £5,000 fine
- **Crown Court** – maximum of seven years' imprisonment and an unlimited fine

There are no automatic civil sanctions contained in CJA 1993. In addition, no contract is automatically void or unenforceable by reason only that it is the result of insider dealing.

3: ASSOCIATED LEGISLATION AND REGULATION

2 MARKET ABUSE AND MANIPULATION

Learning objectives

Know the status of the FCA's Code of Conduct; the territorial scope of the legislation and regulation

Know the offences outlines in the Code of Market Conduct

Know the concept of effect rather than intention; the concept of a reasonable regular user and accepted market practices

2.1 Market abuse

Market abuse is a **civil offence** under **s118 FSMA 2000,** which provides an alternative civil regime for enforcing the criminal prohibitions on insider dealing and misleading statements or impressions.

The UK market abuse rules conform with the **EU Market Abuse Directive**.

The **territorial scope** of market abuse is very wide. It covers everyone, not just authorised firms and approved persons. Firms or persons outside the UK are also covered by the offence.

As market abuse is a **civil offence**, the regulator must prove, on the balance of probabilities, that a person:

- Engaged in market abuse, or
- By taking or refraining from action, required or encouraged another person to engage in market abuses

As shown in the following diagram, there are seven types of behaviour that can amount to market abuse.

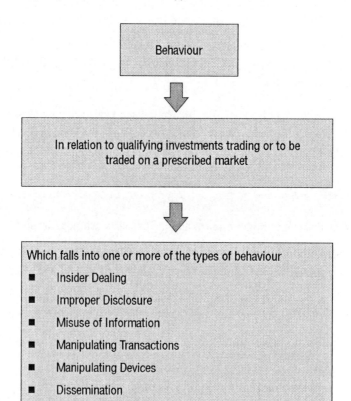

2.2 Requiring and encouraging

Section 123(1)(b) FSMA 2000 allows the regulator to impose penalties on a person who, by taking or refraining from taking any action, has required or encouraged another person or persons to engage in behaviour, which if engaged in by A, would amount to market abuse.

The following are **examples** of behaviour that might fall within the scope of s123(1)(b).

- A director of a company, while in possession of inside information, instructs an employee of that company to deal in qualifying investments or related investments in respect of which the information is inside information. (This could amount to **requiring**.)

- A person recommends or advises a friend to engage in behaviour which, if he himself engaged in it, would amount to market abuse. (This could be **encouraging** market abuse.)

2.3 The regular market user test

A regular user is a **hypothetical reasonable person** who regularly deals on that market in investments of the kind in question. The **regular market user test** then determines in light of the circumstances whether an offence has been committed.

Since the implementation of the Market Abuse Directive, the regular market user is only used to determine whether market abuse has occurred in relation to the behaviours 'Misuse of Information', 'Misleading Behaviour and Distortion'.

Therefore, the regular market user decides:

- Whether information that is not generally available would be relevant when deciding which transactions in qualifying investments or related investments should be undertaken, and

- Whether behaviour is below the expected standard, or creates a false or misleading impression or distorts the market.

2.4 Qualifying investments and prescribed markets

Behaviour will only constitute market abuse if it occurs **in the UK or in relation to qualifying investments traded on a prescribed market**. The term 'behaviour' is specifically mentioned as the offence of market abuse can cover both action and inaction.

A **prescribed market** means any UK RIE, and any regulated market. **Qualifying investment** thus means any investment traded on a UK RIE or a regulated market. **Regulated markets** comprise the main EEA exchanges.

The definition of prescribed market and qualifying investment are amended slightly with reference to the offences of '**Misuse of Information**', '**Misleading Behaviour and Distortion**'. Here, a prescribed market means any UK RIE. Qualifying investment thus means any investment traded on a UK RIE. Therefore, these offences are only relevant to the UK markets.

In addition, the rules confirm that a prescribed market accessible electronically in the UK would be treated as operating in the UK.

As behaviour must be **in relation to** qualifying investments, the regime is not limited to on-market dealings. A transaction in an OTC (Over The Counter) derivative contract on a traded security or commodity would be covered by the regime. In addition, abusive trades on foreign exchanges could constitute market abuse if the underlying instrument also trades on a prescribed market. This makes the regime much wider than the criminal law offences.

2.5 The definition of market abuse

Market abuse is behaviour, whether by one person alone or by two or more persons jointly or in concert, which occurs in relation to:

- Qualifying investments admitted to trading on a prescribed market, or
- Qualifying investments in respect of which a request for admission to trading on a prescribed market has been made, or
- Related investments of a qualifying investment (strictly, this is only relevant to the offences of 'Insider Dealing' and 'Improper Disclosure' – see below)

and falls within one or more of the offences below.

2.6 The seven types of market abuse offence

> **Learning objectives**
>
> **Understand** the statutory offence of market abuse

Now we explain the seven types of behaviour that can constitute market abuse in some more detail.

1. **Insider dealing.** This is where an insider deals, or attempts to deal, in a qualifying investment or related investment on the basis of **inside information**.

2. **Improper disclosure.** This is where an insider discloses **inside information** to another person otherwise than in the proper course of the exercise of his employment, profession or duties.

3. **Misuse of information.** This fills gaps in 1. or 2. above and is where the behaviour is:
   - Based on information which is not generally available to those using the market but which, if available to a regular user of the market, would be regarded by him as relevant when deciding the terms on which transactions in qualifying investments should be effected, and
   - Likely to be regarded by a regular user of the market as a failure on the part of the person concerned to observe the standard of behaviour reasonably expected of a person in his position.

4. **Manipulating transactions.** This consists of effecting transactions or orders to trade (otherwise than for legitimate reasons and in conformity with **accepted market practices**) which:
   - Give, or are likely to give a false or misleading impression as to the supply, demand or price of one or more qualifying investments, or
   - Secure the price of one or more such investments at an abnormal or artificial level.

5. **Manipulating devices.** This consists of effecting transactions or orders to trade which employ fictitious devices or any other form of deception.

6. **Dissemination.** This consists of the dissemination of information by any means which gives, or is likely to give, a false or misleading impression as to a qualifying investment by a person who knew or could reasonably be expected to have known that the information was false or misleading.

7. **Misleading behaviour and distortion.** This fills any gaps in 4., 5. and 6. above and is where the behaviour:
   - Is likely to give a regular user of the market a false or misleading impression as to the supply of, demand for, or price or value of, qualifying investments, or

- Would be regarded by a regular user of the market as behaviour that would distort the market in such an investment and is likely to be regarded by a regular user of the market as a failure on the part of the person concerned to observe the standard of behaviour reasonably expected of a person in his position.

2.7 Intention

The market abuse regime is **effects-based** rather than 'intent-based'. Thus, whether the perpetrator intended to abuse the market is largely irrelevant – the key question is whether the action **did** abuse the market.

2.8 Code of Market Conduct

While the law is set out in FSMA, the regulator (the FCA) also has a duty to draft a **Code of Market Conduct**.

The main provisions of the Code of Market Conduct are that it sets out:

- Descriptions of behaviour that, in the opinion of the regulator, do or do not amount to market abuse. Descriptions of behaviour which do not amount to market abuse are called '**safe harbours**'.
- Descriptions of behaviour that are or are not **accepted market practices** in relation to one or more identified markets.
- Factors that, in the opinion of the regulator, are to be taken into account in determining whether or not behaviour amounts to market abuse.

The Code does not exhaustively describe all types of behaviour that may or may not amount to market abuse.

2.9 Enforcement and penalties

> **Learning objective**
>
> **Understand** the enforcement regime for market abuse

The FCA may impose one or more of the following **penalties** on those found to have committed market abuse.

- An unlimited **fine**
- Issue a **public statement**
- Apply to the court to seek an **injunction** or **restitution order**
- **Disciplinary proceedings**, which could result in withdrawal of authorisation/approval where an authorised/approved person is guilty of market abuse as they will also be guilty of a breach of the FCA's Principles

The case of Paul Davidson ('The Plumber') led to a change in perceptions about how market abuse may be treated.

- For the purposes of the European Convention on Human Rights, market abuse is a **criminal** charge, with a **standard of proof** 'beyond reasonable doubt', and someone committing it is subject to possible criminal prosecution.
- A **civil standard of proof** (on the balance of probabilities) may still be used by the FCA in market abuse cases. Accordingly, the punishment (in accordance with s123 FSMA 2000) is treated as **civil**

for domestic law purposes. However, in the 'Plumber' case, the Tribunal concluded that, where serious matters are involved, a heightened civil standard of proof is necessary, producing a result similar to the criminal standard of proof.

In addition to being able to impose penalties for market abuse, the FCA is given criminal prosecution powers to enforce and impose penalties for insider dealing and market abuse. As previous regulator, the FSA indicated that it would not pursue both the civil and criminal regime. With regard to the enforcement process for market abuse, this is the same as the regulator's disciplinary process.

2.10 Safe harbours

Learning objective	**Know** the statutory exceptions (safe harbours) to market abuse

If a person is within one of the **safe harbours** set out in the **Code of Market Conduct** they are not committing market abuse. These are indicated by the letter **C** in the Handbook.

Generally, there are no rules in the Takeover Code that permit or require a person to behave in a way which amounts to market abuse.

However, the following rules provide a **safe harbour** meaning that behaviour conforming with that rule does not amount to market abuse.

2.10.1 FCA rules

Behaviour caused by the proper operation of a Chinese wall or behaviour that relates to the timing, dissemination or content to a disclosure under the Listing Rules will not amount to market abuse.

2.10.2 Takeover Code

Behaviour conforming with any of the rules of the Takeover Code about the timing, dissemination or content of a disclosure does not, of itself, amount to market abuse. This is subject to the behaviour being expressly required or permitted by a rule and provided it conforms to the General Principles of the Takeover Code.

2.10.3 Buy-back programmes and stabilisation

Behaviour which conforms with the **Buy-Back and Stabilisation Regulation** (in the Market Conduct Sourcebook) will **not** amount to market abuse.

However, buy-back programmes which do not follow the Buy-Back and Stabilisation Regulation are not automatically seen as market abuse, but do not have an automatic safe harbour.

2.11 Due diligence defence

Under s123 FSMA 2000, the regulator may not impose a financial penalty in relation to market abuse where it is satisfied that the person believed, on reasonable grounds, that his behaviour did not amount to market abuse or he took all reasonable precautions and exercised all **due diligence** to avoid engaging in market abuse.

2.12 Notification of suspicious transactions by firms

Learning objective	**Understand** a firm's duty to report suspicious transactions

The Supervision manual in the FCA Handbook (**SUP**) stipulates that an authorised **firm** must **notify the regulator** without delay if it:

- Arranges or **executes** a transaction with or for a client in a qualifying investment admitted to trading on a prescribed market, and
- Has **reasonable grounds** to suspect that the transaction might constitute **market abuse**

Apart from this requirement in respect of **executed** transactions, a firm may voluntarily notify the FCA if there is a suspicious **order** to trade. Note also that Principle for Businesses 11 requires that a firm disclose to its regulator anything of which the regulator would reasonably expect notice.

3 MONEY LAUNDERING

Learning objectives	**Understand** the terms money laundering, criminal conduct and criminal property and the application of money laundering to all crimes and the power of the Secretary of State to determine what is 'relevant criminal conduct'
	Understand that the UK legislation on money laundering is found in the Proceeds of Crime Act 2002 (POCA 2002) as amended by the Serious Organised Crime and Police Act 2005 (SOCPA 2005), the Money Laundering Regulations 2007, the Senior Management Arrangements, Systems and Controls Sourcebook (SYSC) and that guidance to these provisions is found in the Joint Money Laundering Steering Group Guidance Notes and understand the interaction between them

3.1 Overview

Money laundering is the process by which money that is illegally obtained is made to appear to have been legally obtained. By a variety of methods, the nature, source and ownership of these criminal proceeds are concealed.

- Criminal conduct is any crime that constitutes an offence in the UK, or any act abroad that would constitute an offence if it had occurred in the UK.
- Property is criminal property if it constitutes a person's benefit from criminal conduct and the alleged offender knows or suspects that it constitutes this benefit.

This means that UK anti-money laundering legislation applies to the proceeds of all crimes no matter how small.

3.2 Terms and definitions

Learning objective	**Understand** the three stages of money laundering

There are three phases in the laundering of money: **placement**, **layering** and **integration**.

- If the money launderer is able to deposit illicit proceeds within an institution or a State (**placement**), which requires little or no disclosure concerning the ownership of those funds, it may be difficult, if not impossible, to trace the property back to its criminal source.

- In the second instance, if property is passed through a complicated series of transactions (**layering**), involving legitimate as well as illegitimate enterprises, it may again be impossible to identify the owner or origin of that property.

- If the ownership or origin of the funds cannot be ascertained, it is virtually impossible to establish that they are the product of criminal activity. The funds can then be reused in legitimate activity (**integration**).

Legal definitions of the crime of money laundering are as follows.

- The conversion or transfer of property for the purpose of concealing or disguising the origin of the property.

- The concealment or disguise of the true nature, source, location, disposition, movement, rights with respect to, or ownership of, illicitly gained property.

- The acquisition, possession or use of property derived from criminal activity or participation in criminal activity.

These are the definitions employed in the European Union Council Directive of 1991. They have, in the main, been adopted in subsequent UK legislation.

3.3 Action to combat money laundering

In recognition of the scale and impact of money laundering globally, various national governments have in recent years collaborated on an international scale to combat money laundering. Action taken has concentrated not only on the law enforcement process, but also on recommendations to banks and financial institutions to put in place practices and procedures that will assist in the detection of money laundering activity.

In the **EU**, it has been envisaged that the **Money Laundering Directives** would enable the financial sector to play a powerful role in combating money laundering and, consequently, criminal activity. Additionally, it was anticipated that regulation of this kind would maintain public confidence in the soundness and stability of the European financial system.

3.4 EU Money Laundering Directives

In 1991, the EU adopted the **First EU Money Laundering Directive** on the prevention of the use of the financial system for the purpose of money laundering. In part, the impetus for the Directive was the removal of obstacles to free movement of capital and freedom to supply financial services, which was to come about upon completion of the European single market.

The Directive required all EU Member States to create criminal offences applicable to individuals to prohibit money laundering activity. This was enacted into UK legislation via the **Criminal Justice Act 1993 (CJA 1993)**. The money laundering offences within CJA 1993 were later repealed and replaced with the **Proceeds of Crime Act 2002 (POCA 2002)**, which we discuss in detail later.

A **Second Money Laundering Directive** followed in 2001, and the **Third Money Laundering Directive** came into force in **December 2007**. The Third Directive more fully incorporates into EU law the **Forty Recommendations** of the international **Financial Action Task Force (FATF)**.

This requirement of the Directives is enacted into UK legislation by Money Laundering Regulations. The latest **Money Laundering Regulations 2007 (MLR 2007)** repeal earlier regulations and implement the Third Directive.

3.5 Money Laundering Regulations 2007: Institutional liability

> **Learning objective**
>
> **Understand** the main offence set out in the Money Laundering Regulations (internal controls), which includes obligations on firms for adequate training of individuals on money laundering

Under MLR 2007, there are a number of **supervising agencies** with whom businesses of different types are required to register.

- For the purposes of the Regulations, the FCA is responsible for the supervision of authorised firms and also certain other firms including leasing companies, commercial finance providers and safe custody services. Authorised firms are automatically supervised by the FCA but other such businesses must register with the regulator under MLR 2007.

- Various other types of business falling under the regulations are supervised by other authorities: for example, auctioneers accepting cash of €15,000 or more and foreign exchange bureaux must register with HMRC, estate agents must register with the Office of Fair Trading and casinos must register with the Gambling Commission.

- Members of Designated Professional Bodies not conducting mainstream regulated activities are supervised by their professional bodies.

The **Money Laundering Regulations 2007 (MLR 2007)** relate to institutional liability generally. They require internal systems and procedures to be implemented to deter criminals from using certain institutions to launder money. They also aim to enable money laundering to be more easily detected and prosecuted by the law enforcement agencies.

The following 'risk-sensitive' policies and procedures must be established.

- Customer due diligence measures and ongoing monitoring
- Internal reporting
- Record-keeping procedures (for five-year period)
- Internal control
- Risk assessment and management
- Compliance monitoring, management and communication of the policies and procedures
- Recognition of suspicious transactions and reporting procedures (including appointing a Money Laundering Reporting Officer)
- Staff training programmes

Failure to implement these measures is a **criminal offence**. The **FCA** may institute proceedings (other than in Scotland) for money laundering regulation breaches. This power is not limited to firms or persons regulated by the FCA. Whether a breach of the Money Laundering Regulations has occurred is not dependent on whether money laundering has taken place: firms may be sanctioned for not having adequate **anti-money laundering (AML)/ counter-terrorism financing (CTF)** systems.

Failure to comply with any of the requirements of the **MLR** constitutes an offence punishable in the **Crown Court** by a maximum of two years' imprisonment and/or an unlimited fine, or in the **Magistrates' Court** by a maximum six months sentence and a statutory maximum fine of £5,000.

Note that, where a UK business **outsources** certain operations to an overseas jurisdiction, the business is still effectively carried on in the UK. For example, if an investment bank moved its call centre to India, it would still have to comply with money laundering requirements and staff in India would need proper training.

3.6 The Proceeds of Crime Act 2002: Individual liability

> **Learning objective**
>
> **Understand** the main offences of assistance, ie concealing, arrangements, acquisition, use and possession; failure to disclose; tipping off in the regulated sector; and the implications of Part 7 POCA 2002 regarding the objective test in relation to reporting suspicious transactions; that appropriate disclosure (internal for staff and to the National Crime Agency for the firm) is a defence

The three main offences are:

- **Assistance**
- **Failure to disclose**
- **Tipping off**

3.6.1 Assistance (POCA S327-329)

The offence

If any person knowingly helps another person to launder the proceeds of criminal conduct, he or she will be committing an offence. This covers obtaining, concealing, disguising, transferring, acquiring, possessing, investing or using the proceeds of crime. The legislation historically covered the laundering of the proceeds of **serious crime**, however, as a result of the POCA it now covers the proceeds of **all crimes**, no matter how small. This could include evasion of tax.

Possible defences

- It is a defence to the above offence that a person **disclosed** his knowledge or belief concerning the origins of the property either to the police or to the appropriate officer in his firm.

- Under changes made by the **Serious Organised Crime and Police Act 2005 (SOCPA)**, there may also be a defence if the person knew or believed on reasonable grounds that the relevant criminal conduct occurred outside the UK and the conduct was not at the time unlawful in the overseas jurisdiction.

Penalty

The maximum penalties for any offence of assisting a money launderer are **14 years' imprisonment and/or an unlimited fine** in the Crown Court, or six months' imprisonment and a maximum fine of £5,000 in the Magistrates' Court.

3.6.2 Failure to disclose (POCA S330-332)

The offence

If a person discovers information during the course of his employment that makes him **believe or suspect** money laundering is occurring, he must inform the police or the appropriate officer (usually the Money Laundering Reporting Officer (MLRO)) of the firm as soon as possible. If he fails to make the report as soon as is reasonably practicable, he commits a criminal offence.

For those working in the **regulated sector** (for an authorised firm), this offence covers not only where the person had actual suspicion of laundering (ie subjective suspicions) but also where there were **reasonable grounds for being suspicious**. The grounds are when a hypothetical **reasonable person** would in the circumstances have been suspicious (ie **objective suspicions**): this is called the **objective test**.

Possible defences

The only defences to this charge are if a person charged can prove one of the following.

- He had a **reasonable excuse** for failing to disclose this information. Whether an excuse is reasonable will depend on the circumstances of the case, but it is noteworthy that the person charged has the burden of proving that he had a reasonable excuse for his failure to disclose.

- Where the person had no subjective suspicion but is deemed to have objective suspicions, they had not been provided by their employer with appropriate **training** to recognise and report suspicions.

- Under changes made by the Serious Organised Crime and Police Act 2005 (SOCPA), there may also be a defence if the person knew or believed on reasonable grounds that the relevant criminal conduct occurred outside the UK and the conduct was not at the time unlawful in the overseas jurisdiction.

The relevant legislation specifically provides that any person making a disclosure of this kind will not be in breach of any **duty of confidentiality** owed to a customer.

Penalty

This offence is punishable with a maximum of **five years' imprisonment** and/or an **unlimited fine** in the Crown Court, or six months' imprisonment and a maximum fine of £5,000 in the Magistrates' Court.

3.6.3 Tipping off (POCA s333A)

The offence

Even where suspicions are reported, the parties must generally be careful not to alert the suspicions of the alleged launderer since, within the regulated sector, this can itself amount to an offence.

Under s333A, a person within the regulated sector commits an **offence** if, based on information they acquire in the course of business that is likely to prejudice any investigation, they disclose:

- That information has been passed to the police, HMRC, a Nominated Officer (generally, the firm's MLRO) or the **National Crime Agency (NCA)** (formerly, the Serious Organised Crime Agency), or

- That an investigation into money laundering allegations is being contemplated or carried out.

The mischief that s333A seeks to prevent is the mischief of acting so as to frustrate an investigation, and there are a number of **exceptions**. An offence is **not** committed for disclosures within the EEA or territories with anti-money laundering regimes, broadly if the disclosure is:

- Within an EEA financial institution or credit institution or its group

- Between professional advisers within the same group

- Between financial and credit institutions or between advisers generally, for disclosure with the purpose of preventing a money laundering offence

- To the supervisory authority under the Money Laundering Regulations – which, for regulated firms, is the FCA

- By a professional adviser to their client if for the purpose of dissuading the client from committing an offence

Possible defence

It is a defence if the person charged can prove that he neither knew nor suspected that the disclosure would be likely to prejudice an investigation.

3: ASSOCIATED LEGISLATION AND REGULATION

Penalty

Tipping off is punishable with a maximum of **two years' imprisonment** and/or an **unlimited fine** in the Crown Court, or three months' imprisonment and a maximum fine of £5,000 in the Magistrates' Court.

3.6.4 Prejudicing an investigation (POCA s342, as amended)

For a person **outside the regulated sector**, the offence of **prejudicing an investigation** is similar to tipping off. It involves the offence, for those who know or suspect that a money laundering investigation is being carried out, of either:

- In the **non-regulated sector** (s342 (2)(a)), making a disclosure which is likely to prejudice the investigation, or
- For **all persons** (s342 (2)(b)), falsifying, concealing or destroying documents relevant to the investigation

Possible defence

It is a defence if the person charged can prove that he neither knew nor suspected that the disclosure would be likely to prejudice an investigation.

Penalties

Section 342 carries a maximum custodial penalty of **five years** and/or a **fine** in the Crown Court, or six months' imprisonment and a maximum fine of £5,000 in the Magistrates' Court.

3.7 Senior management arrangements, systems and controls (SYSC)

> **Learning objective**
>
> **Understand** the approach covered by the Senior Management Arrangements, Systems and Controls (SYSC), in particular, the systems and controls that the FCA and PRA expects firms to have adopted, the role of the Money Laundering Reporting Officer, Nominated Officer and the compliance function

3.7.1 Systems and controls in relation to compliance, financial crime and money laundering

A firm must take reasonable care to establish and maintain effective systems and controls for compliance with applicable regulations and for countering the risk that the firm might be used to further financial crime. Applicable regulations include the Proceeds of Crime Act 2002, the Money Laundering Regulations 2007 and the Terrorism Act 2000.

The **principles-based approach to regulation** implies that, instead of formulating very detailed rules, the regulator expects firms to work out for themselves how the Principles for Businesses can be given effect in the firm's business.

The systems and controls laid down should enable the firm to identify, assess, monitor and manage **money laundering risk**, which is, the risk that a firm may be used to further money laundering. In addition, the systems and controls should be **comprehensive** and **proportionate** to the **nature**, **scale** and **complexity** of its activities and be regularly assessed to ensure they remain adequate. Failure by a firm to manage money laundering risk will effectively increase the threat to society of crime and terrorism.

In identifying its **money laundering risk** and in establishing the nature of the systems and controls required, a firm should consider a range of factors, including:

- Its customer, product and activity profiles
- Its distribution channels
- The complexity and volume of its transactions

- Its processes and systems
- Its operating environment

The SYSC rules require firms to ensure that their systems and controls include:

- Allocation to a director or senior manager (who may also be the Money Laundering Reporting Officer (MLRO)) overall responsibility within the firm for the **establishment** and **maintenance** of effective anti-money laundering systems and controls.
- Appropriate provision of information to its governing body and senior management, including a report at least annually by that firm's **Money Laundering Reporting Officer (MLRO)** on the operation and effectiveness of those systems and controls.
- **Appropriate training** for its employees in relation to money laundering.
- Appropriate **documentation** of its risk management policies and risk profile in relation to money laundering, including documentation of its application of those policies.
- Appropriate measures to ensure that **money laundering risk** is taken into account in its day-to-day operation eg in the development of new products, the taking on of new customers and changes in its business profile.
- Appropriate measures to ensure that **identification procedures** for customers do not unreasonably deny access to its services to potential customers who cannot reasonably be expected to produce detailed evidence of identity.

3.7.2 The Money Laundering Reporting Officer (MLRO)

The MLRO, which each authorised firm must appoint, has responsibility for oversight of its compliance with the FCA's rules on money laundering.

The **MLRO**:

- Must act as the focal point for all activity within the firm relating to anti-money laundering
- Must have a level of authority and independence within the firm
- Must have access to sufficient resources and information to enable them to carry out that responsibility
- Should be based in the UK

3.7.3 The Nominated Officer

A **Nominated Officer** is someone who has been nominated by their employer to receive reports of suspected money laundering. In practice this will normally be the **MLRO** or **his deputy**.

Employers will have reporting processes in place for staff with suspicions to disclose to the MLRO. The nominated officer will act as a filter for reporting, and is placed under a duty to disclose to the **NCA**, if he knows or suspects, or has reasonable grounds to suspect, that another person is engaged in money laundering.

3.7.4 The compliance function

Depending on the nature, scale and complexity of its business, it may be appropriate for a firm to have a separate **compliance function**. The organisation and responsibilities of the compliance function should be documented.

The compliance function should:

- Be adequately resourced and staffed by an appropriate number of competent staff who are sufficiently independent to perform their duties objectively
- Have unrestricted access to the firm's relevant records
- Have ultimate recourse to its governing body

3: ASSOCIATED LEGISLATION AND REGULATION

A firm which carries on designated investment business with or for customers must allocate to a director or senior manager the function of having responsibility for oversight of the firm's compliance and reporting to the governing body in respect of that responsibility. This will be the person carrying out the controlled function '**Compliance oversight**' under the approved persons regime. As a minimum, this individual will have to oversee compliance with COBS, CASS and COLL.

3.8 Joint Money Laundering Steering Group Guidance

> **Learning objectives**
>
> **Understand** the standards expected by the 2007 JMLSG Guidance Notes particularly in relation to: risk-based approach; requirements for directors and senior managers to be responsible for money laundering precautions; need for risk assessment; need for enhanced due diligence in relation to politically exposed persons; need for high level policy statement; detailed procedures implementing the firm's risk-based approach; financial sanctions regime
>
> **Understand** the Money Laundering aspects of know your customer (Joint Money Laundering Steering Groups' Guidance for the Financial Sector)

3.8.1 Status

The **Joint Money Laundering Steering Group** (JMLSG) is made up of representatives of trade bodies such as the British Bankers Association. The purpose of the guidance notes is to outline the requirements of the UK money laundering legislation, provide a practical interpretation of the MLR 2007 and provide a base from which management can develop tailored policies and procedures that are appropriate to their business.

The current version of the JMLSG Guidance Notes enable the UK financial services industry to take the required **risk-based approach** to the international fight against crime.

The courts must take account of industry guidance, such as the JMLSG Guidance Notes, which have been approved by a Treasury Minister, when deciding whether:

- A person has committed the offence of failing to report money laundering under POCA 2002
- A person has failed to report terrorist financing under the Terrorism Act 2000, or
- A person or institution has failed to comply with any of the requirements of the MLR 2007

When considering whether to take disciplinary action against an authorised firm for a breach of SYSC, the FCA will have regard to whether a firm has followed relevant provisions in the JMLSG Guidance Notes. The guidance will therefore be significant for individuals or companies subject to regulatory action.

The Guidance Notes provide a sound basis for firms to meet their legislative and regulatory obligations when tailored by firms to their particular business risk profile. Departures from good industry practice, and the rationale for so doing, should be documented and may have to be justified to the regulator.

3.8.2 Directors' and senior managers' responsibility for money laundering precautions

Senior management of regulated firms must provide direction to, and oversight of, the firm's **anti-money laundering (AML)** and **counter-terrorism financing (CTF)** systems and controls.

Senior management in regulated firms have a responsibility to ensure that the firm's control processes and procedures are appropriately designed, implemented and effectively operated to manage the firm's risks. This includes the risk of the firm being used to further financial crime.

Senior management of regulated firms must also meet the following specific requirements:

- Allocate to a director or senior manager (who may or may not be the MLRO) overall responsibility for the establishment and maintenance of the firm's AML/CFT systems and controls
- Appoint an appropriately qualified senior member of the firm's staff as the MLRO

3.8.3 High level policy statement and risk-based approach

The regulator requires firms to produce adequate documentation of its risk management policies and risk profile in relation to money laundering, including documentation of the application of those policies.

A statement of the firm's AML/CFT policy and the procedures to implement it will clarify how the firm's senior management intend to discharge their legal responsibility. This will provide a framework of direction to the firm and its staff, and will identify named individuals and functions responsible for implementing particular aspects of the policy. The policy will also set out how senior management makes its assessment of the money laundering and terrorist financing risks the firm faces, and how these risks are to be managed.

The **policy statement** should be tailored to the circumstances of the firm as the use of a generic document might reflect adversely on the level of consideration given by senior management to the firm's particular risk profile.

The policy statement might include, but is not limited to, the following.

Guiding principles
An unequivocal statement of the culture and values to be adopted and promulgated throughout the firm towards the prevention of financial crime
A commitment to ensuring that customers' identities will be satisfactorily verified before the firm accepts them
A commitment to the firm 'knowing its customers' appropriately at acceptance and throughout the business relationship – through taking appropriate steps to verify the customer's identity and business, and his reasons for seeking the particular business relationship with the firm
A commitment to ensuring that staff are trained and made aware of the law and their obligations under it, and to establishing procedures to implement these requirements
Recognition of the importance of staff promptly reporting their suspicions internally

Risk mitigation approach
A summary of the firm's approach to assessing and managing its money laundering and terrorist financing risk
Allocation of responsibilities to specific persons and functions
A summary of the firm's procedures for carrying out appropriate identification and monitoring checks on the basis of their risk-based approach
A summary of the appropriate monitoring arrangements in place to ensure that the firm's policies and procedures are being carried out

3.8.4 The risk-based approach

A **risk-based approach** is mandatory under MLR 2007. The approach requires the full commitment and support of senior management, and the active co-operation of business units. The risk-based approach needs to be part of the firm's philosophy, and as such reflected in its procedures and controls. There needs to be a clear communication of policies and procedures across the firm, together with robust mechanisms to ensure that they are carried out effectively, any weaknesses identified and improvements made wherever necessary.

There are the following **steps** in adopting the required risk-based approach to money laundering.

- Identify the money laundering and terrorist financing risks that are relevant to the firm
- Assess the risks presented by the firm's particular customers, products, delivery channels and geographical areas of operation

- Design and implement controls to manage and mitigate these assessed risks
- Monitor and improve the effective operation of these controls, and
- Record appropriately what has been done, and why

What is the **rationale** of the risk-based approach? To assist the overall objective to prevent money laundering and terrorist financing, a risk-based approach:

- Recognises that the money laundering/terrorist financing threat to firms varies across customers, jurisdictions, products and delivery channels
- Allows management to differentiate between their customers in a way that matches the risk in their particular business
- Allows senior management to apply its own approach to the firm's procedures, systems and controls, and arrangements in particular circumstances, and
- Helps to produce a more cost effective system

3.8.5 Risk assessment and 'Know Your Customer'

Firms are expected to 'know their customers'. The **Know Your Customer (KYC)** requirements:

- Help the firm, at the time customer due diligence is carried out, to be reasonably satisfied that customers are who they say they are, to know whether they are acting on behalf of others, whether there are any government sanctions against serving the customer, and
- Assist law enforcement with information on customers or activities under investigation.

Based on an **assessment of the money laundering / terrorist financing risk** that each customer presents, the firm will need to:

- **Verify the customer's identity (ID)** – determining exactly who the customer is
- **Collect additional 'KYC' information**, and keep such information **current and valid** – to understand the customer's circumstances and business, and (where appropriate) the sources of funds or wealth, or the purpose of specific transactions

Many customers, by their nature or through what is already known about them by the firm, carry a **lower** money laundering or terrorist financing **risk**. These might include:

- Customers who are employment-based or with a regular source of income from a known source which supports the activity being undertaken; (this applies equally to pensioners or benefit recipients, or to those whose income originates from their partners' employment)
- Customers with a long-term and active business relationship with the firm
- Customers represented by those whose appointment is subject to court approval or ratification (such as executors)

Firms should not, however, judge the level of risk solely on the nature of the **customer** or the **product**. Where, in a particular customer/product combination, either or both the customer and the product are considered to carry a higher risk of money laundering or terrorist financing, the overall risk of the customer should be considered carefully. Firms need to be aware that allowing a higher risk customer to acquire a lower risk product or service on the basis of a verification standard that is appropriate to that lower risk product or service, can lead to a requirement for further verification requirements, particularly if the customer wishes subsequently to acquire a higher risk product or service.

3.8.6 Financial Sanctions Regime

There is no single Act of Parliament that sets out the **UK financial sanctions regime**. The regime reflects the requirements of various UN Security Council resolutions, and is implemented by way of EU Regulations and UK Statutory Instruments. There are also EU investment ban and trade sanctions regimes that apply in the UK.

Sanctions can take the form of any of a range of restrictive or coercive measures against selected countries, organisations and individuals. They can include arms embargoes, travel bans, asset freezes, reduced diplomatic links, withdrawal of aid, trade embargoes, and military, sporting and other restrictions. Here we are concerned with financial sanctions, although financial firms need also to keep aware of asset freezes and trade embargoes. The JMLSG gives guidance to the financial services sector on implementing financial sanctions.

A **Consolidated List** of all targets to whom financial sanctions apply is maintained by HM Treasury, and includes all individuals and entities that are subject to financial sanctions in the UK. Each financial sanctions order is set out in a statutory instrument and/or European Community Regulation. This list can be found at: www.hm-treasury.gov.uk/financialsanctions. It is generally a criminal offence directly or indirectly to make funds or economic resources available to or for the benefit of targets on the Consolidated List, or to deal with targets' funds or resources, unless a licence is obtained from HM Treasury.

HM Treasury (HMT) is responsible for implementing, administering and enforcing compliance with UK financial sanctions. In 2007, HMT set up a dedicated **Asset Freezing Unit**, designed to increase the expertise and operational focus that the Government can bring to bear on asset freezing. **Firms must inform HMT's Asset Freezing Unit** as soon as practicable where it has identified an actual match with a person or entity on the HMT list, or where it knows or suspects that a customer or a person with whom the firm has had business dealings has committed a breach, and supply any information that would facilitate compliance.

A person who is in breach of an obligation under a relevant Statutory Instrument will be guilty of an offence unless a defence is successfully made out, and will be liable on conviction to imprisonment and/or a fine. However, in accordance with the Code for Crown Prosecutors, **prosecution** of a firm or individual would only be likely where the prosecuting authorities consider this to be in the public interest, and where they believe that there is enough evidence to provide a realistic prospect of conviction. It is a **defence** for the provider of the funds, economic resources or financial services, not to have known or have had reasonable cause to suspect that the prohibition was being breached.

In line with SYSC, firms should have **proportionate systems and controls** in place to reduce the risk of a breach of UK financial sanctions occurring. Some firms, for example large firms with millions of customers or firms which process many millions of transactions every day, will use automated screening systems. Other firms with smaller numbers of customers and transactions may achieve compliance through other processes.

3.9 Due diligence

One of the most important ways in which money laundering can be prevented is by establishing the identity of clients, thus making it difficult for those trading under assumed names or through bogus companies to gain access to the financial markets. This emphasises the obligation to '**know your customer**'.

In the context of **conduct of business rules**, the firm may generally accept at face value information which customers provide. The **money laundering regulations**, however, require that the firm takes positive steps to verify the information that they receive. The **JMLSG** Guidance Notes lay down some basic, but not exhaustive, procedures that can be followed.

3.10 CDD, EDD and SDD

MLR 2007 requires detailed **customer due diligence (CDD)** procedures and these are explained in the **JMLSG** guidance.

CDD involves:

- Identifying the customer and verifying his identity
- Identifying the beneficial owner (if different from the customer, and taking measures to understand the ownership and control structure, in the case of a company or trust) and verifying his identity
- Obtaining information on the purpose and intended nature of the business relationship

A firm must apply CDD when it:

- Establishes a business relationship
- Carries out an occasional transaction, of €15,000 or more
- Suspects money laundering or terrorist financing
- Doubts the veracity of identification or verification documents

As well as standard CDD there is:

- **Enhanced due diligence (EDD)** – for higher risk situations, customers not physically present when identities are verified, correspondent banking and **politically exposed persons** (**PEPs**)
- **Simplified due diligence (SDD)** – which may be applied to certain financial sector firms, companies listed on a regulated market, UK public authorities, existing child trust funds, and certain pension funds and low-risk products

Firms' information demands from customers need to be '**proportionate**, **appropriate and discriminating**', and to be able to be **justified to customers**.

3.10.1 Enhanced due diligence

EDD measures when a customer is not present include obtaining additional documents, data or information to those specified below, requiring certification by a financial services firm, and ensuring that an initial payment is from a bank account in the customer's name.

The category '**politically exposed persons**' (**PEPs**) comprises higher-ranking **non-UK** public officials, members of parliaments other than the UK Parliament, and such persons' immediate family members and close associates. Prominent PEPs can pose a higher risk because their position may make them vulnerable to corruption. PEPs include of prominent persons. Senior management approval (through an immediate superior) should be sought for establishing a business relationship with such a customer and adequate measures should be taken to establish sources of wealth and of funds.

3.10.2 Simplified due diligence

SDD means not having to apply CDD measures. In practice, this means not having to identify the customer, or to verify the customer's identity, or, where relevant, that of a beneficial owner, nor having to obtain information on the purpose or intended nature of the business relationship.

3.10.3 Evidence of identity

How much identity information to ask for in the course of CDD, and what to verify, are matters **for the judgement of the firm**, based on its **assessment of risk**.

Documents offering evidence of identity are seen in the JMLSG Guidance Notes as forming the following broad hierarchy according to who has issued them, in the following order:

- Government departments or a court
- Other public sector bodies
- Regulated financial services firms
- Other firms subject to MLR or equivalent legislation
- Other organisations

For **private individuals**, the firm should obtain full name, residential address and date of birth of the personal customer. Verification of the information obtained should be based either on a document or documents provided by the customer, or electronically by the firm, or by a combination of both. Where business is conducted face-to-face, firms should request the original documents. Customers should be discouraged from sending original valuable documents by post.

Firms should therefore obtain the following in relation to **corporate clients**: full name, registered number, registered office in country of incorporation, and business address.

The following should also be obtained for private companies:

- Names of all directors (or equivalent)
- Names of beneficial owners holding over 25%

The firm should verify the identity of the corporate entity from:

- A search of the relevant company registry, or
- Confirmation of the company's listing on a regulated market, or
- A copy of the company's Certificate of Incorporation

3.10.4 Ongoing monitoring

> **Learning objective**
>
> **Understand** the importance of ongoing monitoring of business relationships and being able to recognise a suspicious transaction and the requirement of staff to report to the MLRO and for him to report to the National Crime Agency

As an obligation separate from CDD, firms must conduct ongoing **monitoring of the business relationship**, even where SDD applies. Ongoing monitoring of a business relationship includes scrutiny of transactions undertaken including, where necessary, sources of funds.

CDD and **monitoring** is intended to make it more difficult for the financial services industry to be used for money laundering or terrorist financing, but also helps firms guard against fraud, including impersonation fraud.

3.10.5 Reporting of suspicious transactions

All institutions must appoint an 'appropriate person' as the **Money Laundering Reporting Officer (MLRO)**, who has the following functions.

- To receive reports of transactions giving rise to knowledge or suspicion of money laundering activities from employees of the institution

- To determine whether the report of a suspicious transaction from the employee, considered together with all other relevant information, does actually give rise to knowledge or suspicion of money laundering

- If, after consideration, he knows or suspects that money laundering is taking place, to report those suspicions to the appropriate law enforcement agency, the **NCA**

For an individual employee, making a report to the MLRO concerning a transaction means that the employee has fulfilled his statutory obligations and will have **no criminal liability** in relation to any money laundering offence in respect of the reported transaction.

4 Terrorism

4.1 Terrorist activities

> **Learning objectives**
>
> **Know** what activities are regarded as 'terrorism' in the UK (Terrorism Act 2000 Part 1), the obligations on regulated firms under the Counter-Terrorism Act 2008 (money laundering of terrorist funds) and the Anti-Terrorism, Crime and Security Act 2001, Schedule 2, Part 3 (disclosure of information) and where to find the sanction list for terrorist activities
>
> **Understand** the importance of preventative measures in respect of terrorist financing and the essential differences between laundering the proceeds of crime and the financing of terrorist acts and the interaction between the rules of the FCA, the PRA, the Terrorism Act 2000 and the JMLSG Guidance regarding terrorism

Acts of terrorism committed since 2001 have led to an increase in international efforts to locate and cut off funding for terrorists and their organisations.

There is an overlap between the movement of terrorist funds and the laundering of criminal assets. Terrorist groups are often known to have well-established links with organised criminal activity. However, there are two major differences between terrorist and criminal funds.

- Often only small amounts are required to commit a terrorist atrocity, therefore increasing the difficulty of tracking the funds.
- Whereas money laundering relates to the proceeds of crime, terrorists can be funded from legitimately obtained income.

The **Terrorism Act 2000** defines **terrorism** in the UK as the use or threat of action wherever it occurs, designed to influence a government or to intimidate the public for the purpose of advancing a political, religious or ideological cause where the action:

- Involves serious violence against a person, or
- Involves serious damage to property, or
- Endangers a person's life, or
- Creates a serious risk to the health or safety of the public, or
- Is designed to interfere with or seriously disrupt an electronic system, eg a computer virus

4.2 Offences

The Terrorism Act 2000 sets out the following terrorist offences.

- **Fund raising**, which covers inviting another to provide money or other property to fund terrorism
- **Use and possession**, which covers using money or other property for the purposes of terrorism
- **Funding arrangements**, which covers involvement in funding arrangements as a result of which money or other property is made available for terrorism
- **Money laundering**, which covers any arrangement which facilitates the retention or control by any person of terrorist property by means of concealment, removal from the jurisdiction, transfer to nominees or in any other way

An offence will be committed if the action or possession of terrorist funds occurs in the UK. It will also be an offence if the action or possession occurs outside the UK but would have constituted an offence in the UK if it had occurred here.

4.3 Terrorist property

Terrorist property is defined as money or other property which is likely to be used for the purposes of terrorism, proceeds of the commission of acts of terrorism and proceeds of acts carried out for the purposes of terrorism.

4.4 Preventative measures

Although **MLR 2007** focuses on firms' obligations in relation to the prevention of money laundering, **POCA 2000** updated and reformed the obligation to report to cover involvement with any criminal property, and the **Terrorism Act 2000** extended this to cover terrorist property.

The JMLSG Guidance states that the risk of terrorist funding entering the financial system can be reduced if firms apply satisfactory money laundering strategies and, in particular, **know your customer** procedures. Firms should assess which **countries** carry the highest risks and should conduct careful scrutiny of transactions from countries known to be sources of terrorist financing.

For some countries, public information about known or suspected terrorists is available. For example, terrorist names are listed on the US Treasury web site.

4.5 Duty to report terrorism

A **duty to report** occurs where a person believes or suspects that another person has committed a terrorist offence and where the belief or suspicion has arisen in the course of a trade, profession, business or employment.

An individual commits an offence of failing to report if he does not disclose the suspicion and the information on which it is based to a constable (ie the police) as soon as is reasonably practicable.

The following are possible defences to the offence of the failure to report.
- The firm has an established procedure for making disclosures, and the individual properly disclosed the matters in accordance with this procedure.
- The person had a reasonable excuse for not making the disclosure.

A person guilty of failing to report will face a **maximum penalty** of:
- Six months in jail and/or £5,000 fine in the Magistrates Court, or
- Five years in jail and/or an unlimited fine in the Crown Court

4.6 Failure to disclose: regulated sector (s21A Terrorism Act 2000)

In addition to the offences in POCA 2002, there is specific UK legislation relating to terrorism. The main legislation is the **Terrorism Act 2000** which is supplemented by the **Anti-Terrorism Crime and Security Act 2001** and the **Terrorism Act 2000 and Proceeds of Crime Act 2000 (Amendment Regulations) 2007**.

4.6.1 The offence

Under s21A Terrorism Act 2000 (as amended), it is an offence for those working in the **regulated sector** to fail to report (as soon as practicable) knowledge, suspicion or reasonable grounds for suspicion of offences or attempted offences relating to the following.
- Terrorist fund raising
- Use and possession of funds for terrorism
- Arrangements facilitating the retention or control of terrorist property

Thus, as with POCA 2002, there is an **objective test** for reporting. Reports should be made to the police or MLRO as soon as practicable.

4.6.2 Defences

There is a **defence** where person had a **reasonable excuse** for not making such a disclosure, and also where a professional adviser (ie a lawyer, accountant or auditor) receives the information in privileged circumstances.

4.6.3 Penalty

The offence is punishable (as in POCA 2002) with a maximum of **five years' imprisonment and/or an unlimited fine**, or 6 months' imprisonment and a fine of £5,000 in the Magistrates' Court.

4.7 Protected disclosures

There is clearly a concern that where a disclosure is made in accordance with the above requirements the client may claim this is a breach of client confidentiality. However, the rules state that where disclosures are made in accordance with the reporting rules there will not be a breach of client confidentiality.

4.8 Sanctions and the Consolidated List

There are certain customers and organisations who may not be dealt with and whose assets must be frozen, as specified in anti-terrorism legislation and under the financial sanctions regime described earlier in this Chapter.

As indicated earlier, the **Consolidated List** of targets to whom financial sanctions apply is maintained by HM Treasury can be found at: www.hm-treasury.gov.uk/financialsanctions.

4.9 Counter-Terrorism Act 2008

4.9.1 Overview

The **Counter-Terrorism Act 2008 (CTA 2008)** received royal assent and took effect on **26 November 2008**. This legislation is intended to provide further tools in the range of legislation addressing the risks of money laundering, terrorist financing and the proliferation of nuclear, biological, biological or chemical weapons.

4.9.2 Directions

Schedule 7 of CTA 2008 gives powers to the Treasury to issue **directions** to **firms in the financial sector**, which may relate to:

- Customer due diligence
- Ongoing monitoring
- Systematic reporting
- Limiting or ceasing business

The requirements to carry out CDD and ongoing monitoring build on similar obligations under the MLR. The requirements for **systematic reporting** and **limiting or ceasing business** are introduced by CTA 2008.

A Treasury direction under CTA 2008 must relate to a non-EEA country. A **direction** may be given only if the Financial Action Task Force advises that measures be taken, **or** if the Treasury reasonably believes that production or facilitation of nuclear, radiological, biological or chemical weapons, or terrorist financing or

ML activities are being carried on in the country, **and** that this poses a significant risk to UK national interests.

A direction may impose an obligation to carry out EDD, or to undertake **ongoing monitoring** of a business relationship, which may involve retention of documentation or scrutiny of transactions.

Systematic reporting of **prospective transactions** may be required. A firm may also be required not to enter into a specified transaction or business relationship (**limiting or ceasing business**).

4.9.3 Penalties

A failure to comply with a direction can lead to a **civil penalty** (fine) imposed by the FCA as the enforcement authority, or to **criminal prosecution** (carrying a prison term of up to two years and/or a fine) – but not both for the same failure. No civil penalty will be applied and no criminal offence is committed if the firm took all reasonable steps and exercised all due diligence.

5 DISCLOSURE AND TRANSPARENCY

> **Learning objective**
> **Know** the purpose of the Disclosure and Transparency rules and the control of information

5.1 Disclosure and transparency rules (DTR) overview

Disclosure Rules and Transparency Rules (DTR) enforced by the FSA, as previous regulator, were introduced as part of the process of implementation of the **Transparency Directive**, which was completed in January 2007.

DTR requires issuers of securities to **control inside information** and to make timely disclosures of price-sensitive information to the market. DTR includes specific **shareholdings notification** requirements.

5.2 Insider information requirements for companies

There are obligations on companies to manage **access** to and **disclosure** of **inside information**.

The issuer firm must ensure that **employees** with inside information **acknowledge** the legal and regulatory duties entailed.

The firm must establish effective arrangements to **deny access** to inside information to anyone who does not require it to do their job.

There must also be procedures to make a **public disclosure** if the firm cannot ensure confidentiality of information – for example, if they become aware of a breach of confidence.

DTR provides that an issuer may **delay** the **public disclosure** of inside information, such as not to prejudice its legitimate interests, provided that the public would not be likely to be misled and the issuer is able to ensure the confidentiality of the information.

For example, public disclosure of information may be delayed for a limited period if the firm's financial viability in 'grave and imminent danger' to avoid undermining negotiations to ensure the firm's long-term financial recovery.

5.3 Insider lists

Issuers of financial instruments are required by DTR to set up **insider lists** of persons, whether they are employees or not, with access to inside information about the issuer. The list must be **updated** promptly for changes, and must be kept for at least five years.

5.4 The Model Code

> **Learning objective**
>
> **Know** the main purpose and provisions of the Model Code on share dealing by directors and other persons discharging managerial responsibilities including: close periods, undisclosed inside information, Chairman's approval, dealings by the Chairman, short-term dealing, exceptional circumstances, application and record keeping

The **Listing Rules (LR)** set out requirements for issuers with a listing or seeking a listing on a UK regulated market.

LR 9 Annex 1 also contains the **Model Code**. The Model Code restricts dealings by directors and senior executives on their own account in the company's shares at certain times and governs the approval process and disclosure of such dealings at all times: clearance to deal must be sought from the chairman or a designated director. Imposing restrictions that go beyond the law, the Model Code is intended to ensure that directors and senior executives do not abuse, or place themselves under suspicion of abusing, undisclosed **inside information** they may be thought to have, for unfair advantage. No trades should be undertaken in a listed company by its directors in the **close period**.

A listed **company enters a close period 60 days prior to the annual results announcements** (or at the end of the period being reported on, if earlier). Under the transparency rules, a listed company must publish its annual report and accounts within four months of its year end.

In more detail, a company's **close periods** are as follows.

- If there is a preliminary announcement of the company's final results: the **60 days before** the (optional) **preliminary statement** or, if shorter, the period **from the financial year-end** up to the preliminary statement, or

- If there is no preliminary statement: the **60 days before publication of the annual report** or, if shorter, the period from the financial year-end up to the publication of the annual report, and

- For **half-yearly** reports – which must be published within two months of the half-year end – the period **between the half-year end and publication of the report**, and

- For quarterly reporting, the **30 days before** announcement of the **quarterly results** or, if shorter, the period **from the quarter-end** up to the quarterly statement

If, as provided by the **Disclosure and Transparency Rules (DTR)**, **Interim Management Statements** are issued twice-yearly instead of quarterly reports, there is no close period up to the IMS and companies must exercise discretion.

Directors and senior executives of a UK company trading on a regulated market are referred to as **persons discharging managerial responsibilities (PDMRs)** – or **'restricted persons'**. PDMRs and persons connected to them must notify in writing all dealings in the relevant company's shares on their own account to the company within four business days (DTR 3.1.3).

3: ASSOCIATED LEGISLATION AND REGULATION

- Excepting the chairman and chief executive, a director or company secretary or PDMR must not deal in any securities of the company without first **notifying** the chairman or a designated director and receiving **clearance to deal** from him (Model Code).

- In the case of **dealings by the chairman or chief executive**, the chairman or chief executive must receive clearance from each other, or the senior independent director standing in for them, or a board committee or company officer nominated by the chairman or chief executive providing the clearance.

The company must maintain a **record** of the response to any dealing request made by a restricted person (PDMR) and of any **clearance** given. A **copy** of the response and clearance (if any) must be given to the PDMR concerned.

Dealings excluded from the Model Code include take-up of rights issues and takeover offers.

A PDMR must take reasonable steps to prevent any dealings by or on behalf of any connected person of his in any securities of the company on considerations of a **short-term** nature.

PDMRs must seek to prohibit dealings during a **close period** by investment managers or connected persons on behalf of themselves or connected persons.

Outside the close periods, a **PDMR** is however permitted to enter into a **trading plan** (for example, with an independent investment manager) in order to deal in securities of the issuer during both open and prohibited periods without breaching the Model Code and without suspicion of dealing on the basis of **inside information**.

A PDMR who does not possess inside information may be given clearance by the designated director to sell (but not to buy) the company's securities if there are **exceptional circumstances** such as severe financial difficulty – for example, if he has a pressing financial commitment which cannot be satisfied otherwise, or if there has been a court order requiring the PDMR to sell or transfer the securities. The Model Code states that the regulator should be consulted at an early stage about any application by a PDMR to deal in exceptional circumstances.

A **breach** of the Model Code will result in disciplinary action being taken by the UKLA. This action may be taken against the individual or the company. The Model Code is not part of the law and breach of the Code does not constitute a criminal offence.

DTR also covers notifications of holdings of PDMRs and connected persons in a company's shares. The rules require those who discharge managerial responsibilities to make notifications of their own account transactions in the company's securities to the issuer and the market via a Regulatory Information Service.

6 DATA PROTECTION AND RECORD-KEEPING

> **Learning objective**
>
> **Know** the eight Data Protection principles, the need for notification of data controllers with the Information Commissioner; the record-keeping requirements of FCA-regulated firms

6.1 Data Protection Act 1998

Under the **Data Protection Act 1998 (DPA 1998)**, where persons process personal data, whether electronically or manually, they must (unless exempt) be registered with the **Information Commissioner** (who maintains a **public registry of data controllers**) and must comply with the DPA provisions. The requirements apply to most organisations and cover all personal data whether it relates to clients, employees, suppliers or any other person. In essence, to comply with DPA 1998, firms should be open with individuals about information held about them and very careful about passing that information to third parties.

3: ASSOCIATED LEGISLATION AND REGULATION

6.2 Data Protection Principles

Under DPA 1998, there are **eight Data Protection Principles** (sometimes called the principles of good information handling) with which those controlling personal data must comply.

- **Principle 1** – Personal data shall be **processed fairly and lawfully**. This requires that data shall not be processed unless consent has been obtained from the subject of the data, or the processing is necessary to comply with legal obligations or to protect the vital interests of the subject of the data. Protection of vital interests could be where medical details need to be passed as a result of an accident. Also, where the data is 'sensitive personal data' (eg regarding ethnic origin, religion, health, or criminal record) additional requirements are imposed to handle such data.

- **Principle 2** – Personal data shall be obtained only for specified and lawful purposes and shall only be processed in a manner that is compatible with those purposes.

- **Principle 3** – Personal data shall be **adequate, relevant and not excessive** in relation to the purpose or purposes for which they are processed. This is to ensure no more data is held on a person than is strictly required in the circumstances.

- **Principle 4** – Personal data shall be **accurate** and, where necessary, kept up-to-date. This requires reasonable steps to be taken to ensure the accuracy of the data.

- **Principle 5** – Personal data processed for any purpose(s) shall **not be kept for longer** than is necessary for that purpose(s). Data should be reviewed regularly to determine whether it can be deleted.

- **Principle 6** – Personal data shall only be processed in accordance with data subjects, ie in accordance with the wishes of those individuals who are the subjects of the data.

- **Principle 7** – Appropriate **technical and organisational measures** shall be taken against unauthorised or unlawful processing of personal data and against accidental loss or destruction of, or damage to, personal data. Consideration should therefore be taken as to those members of staff accessing data and the technology used to store such data.

- **Principle 8** – Personal data shall **not be transferred** to a country or territory outside the **EEA**, unless that country or territory ensures an adequate level of protection of the rights and freedoms of data subjects in relation to the processing of personal data. Guidance as to which countries comply with these requirements can be obtained from the Information Commissioner.

6.3 Breaches of the Principles

Where breaches occur, the **Information Commissioner** has **wide powers** to issue enforcement notices requiring the data controller to take certain action to remedy any breaches.

- Breaches of the DPA 1998 requirements are punishable by a maximum fine of **£5,000** in the **Magistrates' Court** and **unlimited fines** in the **Crown Court**.

- There are also powers to enter premises and seize documents with a court warrant.

6.4 Record-keeping: general rules for firms

A firm must take reasonable care to make and retain adequate records of matters and dealings (including accounting records) which are the subject of requirements and standards under the regulatory system.

Records should be capable of being reproduced in English, on paper, or alternatively in the official language of a different country for records relating to business done there.

As already mentioned, MiFID requires firms to keep records for **five years**, for MiFID business generally.

For **non-MiFID business**, a retention period of five years also commonly applies, but there are some exceptions, including the following.

Record retention periods

- Indefinitely, for records relating to pension transfers, pension opt-outs and FSAVCs (Free-Standing Additional Voluntary Contributions arrangements, for pensions)
- Six years for financial promotions for life policies and pension contracts
- Three years for non-MiFID suitability records for products other than pension transfers, pension opt-outs, FSAVCs, life policies and personal and stakeholder pension contracts
- Three years, for copies of confirmations and periodic statements, in respect of non-MiFID business
- Three years, for periodic statements provided to participants in collective investment schemes
- Six months for records of telephone conversations and electronic communications

6.5 Record-keeping and DPA 1998

As a result of DPA 1998, authorised firms should be aware that **records** required to be obtained and kept under FCA rules (including money laundering identification requirements) must also comply with the requirements of DPA 1998.

7 PRUDENTIAL STANDARDS

> **Learning objectives**
>
> **Know** the purpose of the capital adequacy requirements
>
> **Know** the purpose, scope and application of the liquidity framework requirements and how they apply to regulated firms

7.1 Capital adequacy requirements

The financial regulation of **capital adequacy** seeks to enhance investor protection. The rules seek to ensure that a firm always has **'adequate financial resources'** – ie, enough capital to operate.

If a firm is forced to maintain significant capital resources to remain in business, it means that there should be enough money to close down the business and transfer positions in an orderly manner, should it go into liquidation. Associated with these rules are requirements on **reporting, notification** and **internal controls**.

Adequate financial resources and adequate systems and controls are necessary for the effective management of **prudential risks** – that is, the risk that the firm becomes financially unsound.

The overall aim of **capital requirements** rules is to ensure that firms remain solvent by having greater assets at their command than they will need to cover their positions. In general, a firm must maintain, at all times, financial resources in excess of its financial resources requirement.

The requirements amplify **Principle for Businesses 4**, which states that a firm must maintain adequate financial resources.

Under the re-structured regulatory system, the **PRA** is the **prudential regulator** of **'prudentially significant' firms** – banks and building societies, credit unions, insurers, and some investment firms. Note that the FCA is the **conduct regulator** of these firms, and so such firms are subject to **'dual regulation'**. The **FCA** is responsible for **prudential and liquidity regulation** of **non-dual regulated firms**.

7.2 Capital adequacy requirements

The UK financial resources requirements for major firms are based on the **Basel Capital Accords**, developed by the **Basel Committee on Banking Supervision**.

The second Basel Accord, Basel II, is implemented in the European Union via the **Capital Requirements Directive (CRD)** for internationally active credit institutions and investment firms. The CRD directly affects banks, building societies and certain types of investment firm in the UK. The Directive is designed to require firms to ensure that they have financial resources in excess of their financial resources requirement.

The CRD framework consists of three '**pillars**'.

- **Pillar 1** sets out the minimum capital requirements firms are required to meet for credit, market and operational risk
- **Pillar 2:** firms and regulatory supervisors have to take a view on whether a firm should hold additional capital against risks not covered in Pillar 1 and must take action accordingly
- **Pillar 3** aims to improve market discipline by requiring firms to publish certain details of their risks, capital and risk management

The **Basel Committee on Banking Supervision** does not have legal powers but creates common standards and guidelines of best practice with the aim that individual States will implement these in their own law. The Committee has tried to reduce divergences in international supervisory standards. They seek to ensure that all foreign banking establishments are actually supervised by someone and that supervision is adequate.

Investment firms which are subject to the risk-based capital requirements of the CRD are subject to the **General Prudential sourcebook (GENPRU)** and the **Prudential Sourcebook for Banks, Building Societies and Investment Firms (BIPRU)**.

For **personal investment firms (PIFs)** not subject to the CRD, a **capital resources requirement** comprising an **expenditure-based requirement (EBR)** with a **minimum capital resources** floor of £20,000 (double the current level of £10,000) is being phased in as follows:

- End of 2013 – PIFs should hold a minimum of one-month EBR (minimum capital floor £15,000)
- End of 2014 – PIFs should hold a minimum of two-months EBR (minimum capital floor £15,000), subordinated loans restricted to 400%
- End of 2015 – PIFs should hold a minimum of three-months EBR (minimum capital floor £20,000), subordinated loans restricted to 200%

The required capital resources must be held in realisable assets such as cash. The regulator does not want firms to be completely reliant on debt funding and so will allow the inclusion of subordinated debt in the capital resources calculation, but subject to a limit on gearing.

7.3 Basel II and Basel III

Basel II aimed to make the framework more risk-sensitive and more representative of modern banks' risk management practices. The new framework aims to leave the overall level of capital held by banks collectively broadly unchanged.

The **capital adequacy framework** is intended to reduce the probability of consumer loss or market disruption as a result of prudential failure. It does so by seeking to ensure that the financial resources held by a firm are commensurate with the risks associated with the business profile and the control environment within the firm.

In the light of the **banking and financial crisis of the late 2000s**, some considered the Basel II regime partly to have led to the problems because it is a rule-driven system based on 'letter rating' of risks and is arguably, by its nature, backward-looking.

Basel III is the name given to an update to the Basel Accords. Basel III introduces more stringent requirements on banks, including counter-cyclical capital buffers, and introduces new regulatory requirements on bank liquidity and bank leverage. Basel III is expected to be implemented in stages over a transition period from 2013 to 2021.

Basel III regulations include:

- Tighter definitions of common equity, with a requirement for banks to hold 4.5% by January 2015 (compared with 2.0% currently), then a further capital conservation buffer of 2.5% to withstand future periods of stress, totalling 7%
- A framework for counter-cyclical capital buffers, with banks having a capital ratio below 2.5% facing restrictions on dividends, buybacks and bonuses
- Measures to limit counterparty credit risk
- Short- and medium-term quantitative liquidity ratios
- The introduction of an internationally harmonised leverage ratio, acting as a backstop to risk-based capital measures

Basel III is intended to enhance the transparency of banks' capital base, which is categorised into:

- **Tier 1 capital**: predominantly ordinary shares and retained earnings
- **Tier 2 capital**: includes long-term subordinated debt and revaluation reserves
- **Tier 3 capital**: includes short-term subordinated debt (Tier 3 will be abolished to ensure that market risks are met with the same quality of capital as credit and operational risks)

Major banks are already moving to comply with the Basel III rules ahead of its deadlines, with many banks attempting to meet the standards by 2013. This is seen as helping to demonstrate to investors that a bank is financially strong.

In January 2012, it was stated that banks would be required to hold easily sold assets as **liquidity buffers** from 2015, but would be allowed to dip into these buffers at times of stress. (These buffers are therefore unlike Basel capital standards, for which falling below thresholds puts a bank at immediate risk of being shut down or nationalised.) There were pleas from the industry for a delay or a substantial re-write of the **liquidity coverage ratio (LCR)** which had proved to be controversial. The LCR rules require banks to maintain buffers against a 30-day crisis.

In **January 2013**, the Group of Governors and Heads of Supervision (GHOS) agreed to **delay the LCR requirements** by a further **four years**. Additionally, banks will be permitted to select from a longer list of approved assets including some equities and securitised mortgage debt in building up liquidity buffers for use in a financial crisis. Banks will now have to meet 60% of the LCR obligations by 2015, with the full rule being phased in annually through to **2019**.

Failure by the **US** to provide a firm date for introducing its Basel III regulations has, in late 2012, led to some commentators, particularly in France, doubting the US's commitment to the reform programme.

While the Basel process has traditionally operated by consensus and persuasion, a more aggressive implementation process is planned for Basel III. **'Global review teams'** will be sent across the globe to check that the standards are being implemented. **Thematic reviews** are being established – for example, on how banks measure the riskiness of assets – to check whether the rules are delivering the same outcomes in different countries.

7.4 Liquidity requirements

7.4.1 Introduction

Regulatory liquidity requirements are concerned with the adequacy of the financial resources that a firm needs to hold in order to be able to meet its liabilities as they fall due.

Firms must consider different **liquidity risk mitigation tools**, including a system of limits and liquidity buffers in order to be able to withstand a range of different stress events and an adequately diversified funding structure and access to funding sources.

The firm must adjust its strategies, internal policies and limits on liquidity risk and develop an effective **contingency funding plan**, taking into account the outcome of alternative stress test scenarios. The contingency funding plan should be able to address possible liquidity shortfalls in emergency situations, ensuring that the firm has sufficient liquidity resources to enable the firm to meet its liabilities as they fall due.

7.4.2 The overall liquidity adequacy rule

The over-arching **liquidity adequacy rule** (BIPRU 12.2.1) states that: 'A firm must at all times maintain **liquidity resources** which are adequate, both as to amount and quality, to ensure that there is no significant risk that its liabilities cannot be met as they fall due.'

The liquidity resources that can be made available **by other members of the firm's group** must not be counted. Resources made available through **emergency liquidity assistance from a central bank** must also be excluded.

Foreign firms with UK branches may only include liquidity resources which meet certain conditions: the resources must be unencumbered, under day-to-day control of the senior management of the UK branch, held in the sole name of the UK branch, and attributed to the balance sheet of the UK branch.

7.4.3 Individual liquidity adequacy assessments

Investment firms must carry out an **Individual Liquidity Adequacy Assessment (ILAA)**, based on stress testing, at least annually. The regulator will generally request to see the ILAA as part of the ongoing supervisory process.

Stress tests must be based on the following scenarios.

- **Idiosyncratic liquidity stress.** This stress considers an unforeseen name- or firm-specific shock liquidity stress, where the market and / or retail depositors perceive the firm to be unable to meet its liabilities as they fall due for a period of two weeks, followed by a longer-term stress (out to three months from the inception of the stress) of the severity of a multi-notch credit rating downgrade that results in the crystallisation of liabilities linked to the firm's credit rating.

- **Market-wide liquidity stress.** This stress considers an unforeseen short-term market-wide dislocation that gradually evolves into a long-term market-wide liquidity stress, where there are widespread concerns about the solvency of financial sector firms and uncertainty about the value of financial assets. As a result, there is likely to be a very high degree of illiquidity in financial markets for a period of two weeks, followed by a gradual improvement in market conditions over a period of three months form the inception of the stress.

- **Combined idiosyncratic and market-wide liquidity stress.** Under this stress, the firm's ILAA considers a combination of a market-wide and firm-specific liquidity stresses. The firm must consider this as a separate stress test and not merely as a summation of the idiosyncratic and market-wide stresses, because their interaction and any resulting mitigating actions firms could take will be different.

7.4.4 Liquid assets buffer

Investment firms must maintain a **liquid assets buffer** made up of high quality, unencumbered assets, in most cases comprising:

- High quality debt securities of governments or central banks
- Securities issued by certain designated development banks, such as the European Bank for Reconstruction and Development, and the African Development Bank
- Reserves in the form of sight deposits with specified central banks, comprising the EEA States, Australia, Canada, Japan, Switzerland and the USA

7.4.5 Overarching liquidity systems and controls requirements

Firms must have in place '**robust strategies, policies, processes and systems**' that are comprehensive and proportionate to the nature, scale and complexity of the firm's activities. These strategies, policies, processes and systems must enable the firm to identify, measure, manage and monitor liquidity risk, as well as to enable it to assess and maintain on an ongoing basis the amounts, types and distribution of liquidity resources that it considers adequate to cover:

- The nature and level of the liquidity risk to which it is or might be exposed, and
- The risk that the firm cannot meet its liabilities as they fall due

For investment firms in general (but subject to certain exemptions, including firms dealing only on their own account), the systems should also assess the resources needed to cover the risk that its liquidity resources might in the future fall below the level, or differ from the quality and funding profile, of those resources advised as appropriate by the regulator in that firm's individual liquidity guidance or, for firms with a simpler business model, a simplified buffer requirement.

8 REGULATION THROUGH EUROPEAN DIRECTIVES

8.1 Markets in Financial Instruments Directive (MiFID)

> **Learning objective**
> **Know** the relevant European Union Directives and the impact on the UK financial services industry in respect of: passporting within the EEA (MiFID); home v host state regulation (MiFID)

8.1.1 Overview

The **Markets in Financial Instruments Directive (MiFID)** was adopted by the European Council in April 2004 and is part of the European **Financial Services Action Plan**. After delays, MiFID eventually became effective on **1 November 2007**.

MiFID replaced the previous Investment Services Directive (ISD), and it applies to all **investment firms**, eg investment and retail banks, brokers, assets managers, securities and futures firms, securities issuers and hedge funds.

Although MiFID has extended regulation beyond what was regulated under the ISD, a significant part of the **retail financial services sector** falls outside the scope of MiFID.

The following are also **excluded** from the scope of MiFID.

- **Insurance companies** including reinsurers
- **Pension funds** and **collective investment schemes**, and their depositories or managers, although UCITS managers who provide advice or discretionary management to clients who are not funds will generally be subject to MiFID requirements
- **Group treasury activities**
- **Persons administering their own assets**
- **Professional investors** investing only for themselves
- **Commodity producers and traders**
- Investment services relating to administration of **employee share schemes**
- **Incidental business in the course of professional activity** bound by legal, ethical or regulatory provisions
- **Firms not providing investment services** or involved in investment activities

MiFID applies to **EEA-domiciled firms** only. (However, the regulatory rules extend MiFID requirements to '**MiFID equivalent activities of third country firms**'.)

8.1.2 Scope of MiFID

MiFID applies to a specified range of 'core' **investment services and activities** in relation to specified categories of **financial instruments**, as summarised below.

- **Investment firms** are firms which provide such services or engage in such activities.
- Investment firms are also regulated in respect of various 'non-core' **ancillary services** they may provide (as also listed below).
- **Credit institutions** (which includes banks and building societies, in the UK) are regulated by the Banking Consolidation Directive. However, most MiFID provisions apply to these institutions when they engage in activities within MiFID's scope.

Investment services and activities

- Receiving and transmitting orders
- Execution of orders on behalf of clients
- Dealing on own account
- Managing portfolios on a discretionary basis
- Investment advice
- Underwriting of financial instruments
- Placing of financial instruments
- Operating a Multilateral Trading Facility (MTF)

Financial instruments covered by MiFID

- Transferable securities, eg shares and bonds
- Money market instruments
- Units in collective investment undertakings
- Derivatives relating to securities, currencies, interest rates and yields, financial indices and financial measures settled either physically or in cash, including: options, futures, swaps and forward rate agreements

- Commodity derivatives capable of being settled in cash, or capable of being physically settled on a regulated market or MTF, and certain other commodity derivatives are not for commercial purposes
- Derivative instruments for transferring credit risk
- Financial CfDs
- Derivatives relating to climatic variables, freight rates, emission allowances, inflation rates or other official economic statistics capable of being settled in cash

Ancillary services

- Safekeeping, custodianship and administration of financial instruments
- Granting credit or loans to an investor for a transaction in which the firm is involved
- Advising undertakings on capital structure, industrial strategy
- Advising on mergers and acquisitions
- Foreign exchange services connected with providing investment services
- Investment research, financial analysis or other general recommendations

8.1.3 Passporting within the EEA

The idea of a '**passport**', which already existed before MiFID, enables firms to use their domestic authorisation to operate not only in their **Home State**, but also in other **Host States** within the **European Economic Area** (EEA) (EU plus Norway, Iceland and Liechtenstein).

An important aspect of MiFID is that, to make cross-border business easier, the home country principle has been extended. Under MiFID, investment firms are authorised by the Member State in which their registered office is located (the **Home State**).

MiFID has extended the **range of activities that can be passported** to include:

- Investment advice
- Operating a Multilateral Trading Facility (MTF)
- Investment activities relating to commodity derivatives, credit derivatives and CfDs
- Investment research, where it is ancillary to a different core service
- Some underwriting activities

Where a **branch** is set up, **Host State** rules will continue to apply. A **tied agent** established in the EEA will be able to act on behalf of a firm instead of the firm needing to set up a branch. (A '**tied agent**', similarly to an **appointed representative** under FSMA 2000, acts on behalf of, and under the authority of, an investment firm and as a result does not require authorisation.)

Where a firm makes use of a passport:

- **Organisational matters** will be regulated by the **home state**: these include authorisation, fitness and propriety, capital adequacy, Principles for Businesses, senior management arrangements, systems and controls, client assets including client money, conflicts of interest, personal account dealing (as covered in the conduct of business rules, COBS), investment research (COBS), transaction reporting and transparency, and compensation arrangements.
- **Operational matters**, for example conduct of business rules which are not 'organisational matters' will be regulated by:
    - The **host state**, for activities of a branch 'within its territory'
    - The **home state**, for cross-border services

8.2 UCITS: Collective investment schemes

> **Learning objective**
>
> **Know** relevant European regulation: selling cross-border collective investment schemes

8.2.1 UCITS Directives

The EU has enacted a number of directives relevant to collective investment schemes (CISs). These are known as the **UCITS Directives**. **UCITS** stands for **Undertakings for Collective Investment in Transferable Securities**.

The aim of UCITS was to create a type of passport throughout the EEA for collective investment schemes that meet the UCITS criteria. The idea was to promote the free movement of services in the same way that investment firms can passport their services throughout the EEA.

The CIS must be authorised in its home State and receive confirmation from its home State regulator that the CIS complies with UCITS criteria. That confirmation is then provided to the host State regulator, who the fund manager notifies that they wish to market the fund in that EEA State. Although UCITS aims to make cross-border sales of CISs easier, the CIS must comply with the marketing rules of the host State and the documentation requirements of the Directive.

In the first **UCITS Directive**, the definition of **permitted investments** was very narrow. UCITS was updated in 2002 by the **UCITS III Product Directive,** which expanded the range of assets that UCITS funds are able to invest in. It also made provision for a single UCITS scheme to replace all of the previous categories of fund which had separate rules.

UCITS IV, implemented in mid-2011, enhances the UCITS regime. The changes introduced include a new passport for management companies and a new point-of-sale consumer disclosure document (Key Investor Information' or KII) to provide investors with clearer and more concise information to help their decision-making.

8.2.2 UCITS schemes

As a result of the **UCITS Product Directive**, UCITS schemes are now able to invest in the following types of **permitted investment**.

- Transferable securities (see below)
- Money market instruments
- Forward contracts and financial derivatives
- Deposits
- Units in other UCITS and regulated non-UCITS Collective Investment Schemes

Transferable securities comprise shares, instruments creating or acknowledging indebtedness (eg debentures, loan stock, bonds, government and public securities) and certificates representing certain securities.

Although **commodity derivatives** are excluded, it would appear that derivatives based on commodity indices could be eligible as financial derivatives.

> **Exam tip**: A common exam question is about commodity derivatives being outside the scope of UCITS schemes.

8.3 The Prospectus Directive

| Learning objective | **Know** the relevant European regulation: selling securities cross-border (Prospectus Directive) |

The EU's **Prospectus Directive** (2003) was implemented in the UK by the Prospectus Regulations 2005, which amended Part IV FSMA 2000, and by the Prospectus Rules in the regulatory Handbook.

The Directive requires that a prospectus is produced when there is a public offer of securities or where securities are admitted to trading on an EU regulated market. This provision casts a wider net than listings, since it covers securities traded on 'second' markets and through other trading facilities. The Directive specifies the content of prospectuses and requires that they are approved by the relevant national regulator.

These requirements are designed to increase protection of investors by ensuring the quality of prospectuses and to enhance international market efficiency through the issue of single approved prospectuses for use throughout the EEA. Investors must be given 'essential and appropriately structured' information for them to understand the nature of the risks posed by the issuer.

Under the Prospectus Directive, there is a '**single passport**' for issuers, with the result that a prospectus approved by one competent authority can be used across the EEA without any further approval or burdensome administrative procedures in other Member States. If the competent authority in the relevant member state approves the prospectus, it will be accepted throughout the EEA.

The overall position is that a prospectus is required in the case of an offer of transferable securities to the public in the EEA, unless an exemption applies. An 'offer' is defined broadly and covers any communication in any form and by any means which presents sufficient information about the terms of the offer and the securities offered such as to enable an investor to decide to buy or subscribe to those securities.

There are exemptions to the Prospectus Directive, for example for smaller offers, and for offers made only to qualified investors, a category that aligns with the MiFID categorisations of eligible counterparties and professional clients.

3: ASSOCIATED LEGISLATION AND REGULATION

CHAPTER ROUNDUP

- To act on information not freely available to the market is to commit the criminal offence of insider dealing.

- Various types of behaviour, including insider dealing and manipulation of transactions, can constitute market abuse. The Code of Market Conduct describes behaviours that amount to market abuse.

- Money laundering has three stages: placement, layering, integration. Those in the financial services industry must keep alert to possible offences relating to the proceeds of any crime.

- Joint Money Laundering Steering Group guidance requires firms to assess risks when implementing money laundering precautions. The 'Know Your Customer' principle implies that firms should, where appropriate, take steps to find out about the customer's circumstances and business.

- It is a criminal offence to assist laundering the proceeds of crime, to fail to report it satisfactorily, or to tip-off someone laundering the proceeds of crime. Firms should have systems and controls in place that are designed to avoid breaching financial sanctions against individuals or entities.

- The Money Laundering Regulations 2007 apply to all authorised firms and individuals. Each firm must have a Nominated Officer (MLRO), who will decide whether to report suspicions to the National Crime Agency.

- Fund raising, use and possession, funding arrangements and money laundering are offences under the Terrorism Act 2000. There is a duty to report suspected terrorism to the police.

- The Disclosure and Transparency Rules (DTR) require issuers of securities to control access to inside information and to make disclosures of price-sensitive information to the market on a timely basis.

- The UK Listing Authority imposes rules for listed company directors in the Model Code, which should not be undertaken during close periods or for the short term.

- Those who process personal data must be registered with the Information Commissioner.

- The Data Protection Act 1998 sets out eight Data Protection Principles with which data controllers must comply. The principles are designed to ensure that firms are open with individuals about the information they hold about them, and should be careful about passing it on.

- Capital adequacy rules are designed to enhance investor protection by ensuring that a firm always has enough capital to operate.

- The Markets in Financial Instruments Directive (MiFID) replaced the Investment Services Directive (ISD), with effect from 1 November 2007. MiFID applies to all investment firms, including investment banks, securities dealers and portfolio managers.

- Under MiFID, firms are authorised by the Member State in which they their registered office is located. Where a branch is set up, Host State rules will continue to apply. 'Passporting' enables them to operate throughout the EEA.

- UCITS Directives enable passporting for collective investment schemes which meet UCITS criteria, in the interests of facilitating cross-border financial services within Europe. The scheme must be regulated or authorised in its Home State, and the home State regulator will confirm that the scheme complies with UCITS criteria.

- In the interests of investor protection, the Prospectus Directive imposes disclosure standards when there is an offer of securities. A Prospectus which is formally approved in one EEA member state can be used across the EEA without further approval: this is referred to as the 'single passport' for issuers.

3: ASSOCIATED LEGISLATION AND REGULATION

Test Your Knowledge

Check your knowledge of the chapter here, without referring back to the text.

1.	What criminal legislation covers insider dealing?	
2.	What is the definition of an insider under criminal law?	
3.	What is the maximum penalty for market abuse?	
4.	What are the three stages of money laundering?	▪ ▪ ▪
5.	What legislation makes it a criminal offence for an individual to assist a money launderer?	
6.	What is the maximum penalty for assisting a money launderer?	
7.	Explain what is meant by the 'Nominated Officer' in money laundering prevention provisions.	
8.	A direction by HM Treasury under the Counter-Terrorism Act 2008 must relate to a threat to the UK from within the EEA. True or False?	
9.	Outline the restrictions imposed by the Model Code.	
10.	Which body or person maintains a register of data controllers under the Data Protection Act 1998?	

3: ASSOCIATED LEGISLATION AND REGULATION

11.	Outline how 'home State' and 'host State' rules apply under MiFID.	
12.	What is the effect of the 'single passport' under the Prospectus Directive?	

Test Your Knowledge: Answers

1. The Criminal Justice Act 1993.

   (See Section 1.1)

2. Under CJA 1993, an insider is an individual who knowingly has inside information and knows it is from an inside source.

   (See Section 1.2)

3. An unlimited fine. Other sanctions also include a public statement, an injunction or restitution order.

   (See Section 2.9)

4. Placement, layering and integration.

   (See Section 3.2)

5. The Proceeds of Crime Act 2002.

   (See Section 3.6)

6. Fourteen years in prison and/or an unlimited fine.

   (See Section 3.6.1)

7. The Nominated Officer is someone who has been nominated by their employer to receive reports of suspected money laundering. In practice this will be the Money Laundering Reporting Officer (MLRO) or his deputy.

   (See Section 3.7.3)

8. False. The opposite is true. A Treasury direction under CTA 2008 must relate to a non-EEA country.

   (See Section 4.9.2)

9. The Model Code restricts listed company directors and senior executives from dealing in their companies' without clearance (normally from the Chairman of the company), and from dealing in close periods. The Code is intended to ensure that directors and senior executives do not abuse, or place themselves under suspicion of abusing, undisclosed inside information they may be thought to have, for unfair advantage.

   (See Section 5.4)

10. The Information Commissioner.

    (See Section 6.1)

11. Under MiFID, investment firms are authorised by the Member State in which their registered office is located and home State rules will apply. Where a branch is set up, host State rules will however apply.

    (See Section 8.1.2)

12. The 'single passport' concept means that a prospectus approved by one competent authority can be used across the EEA without any further approval or burdensome administrative procedures in other Member States.

    (See Section 8.3)

4 FCA Conduct of Business and Client Assets Sourcebooks

INTRODUCTION

The Principles for Businesses are central to the 'principles-based' approach to regulation. The regulator has made detailed rules in the Conduct of Business Sourcebook (COBS) which are aimed largely at providing such protection.

The COBS rules cover a wide range of operational areas, and were substantially revised in 2007 following the implementation of the Markets in Financial Instruments Directive (MiFID). This underlines the fact that regulation is increasingly being determined at the European level.

COBS was transferred from the FSA Handbook to the new FCA Handbook with effect from 1 April 2013.

CHAPTER CONTENTS

		Page
1	COBS: Application and General Provisions	123
2	Accepting Customers	125
3	Communications with Clients	130
4	Advising and Selling	134
5	Dealing and Managing	137
6	Reporting to Clients	148
7	Client Assets Rules	149
8	COBS Summary	155
	Chapter Roundup	160
	Test Your Knowledge	161

4: FCA CONDUCT OF BUSINESS AND CLIENT ASSETS SOURCEBOOKS

LEARNING OBJECTIVES

Application and general provisions of the FCA Conduct of Business Sourcebook

- **Know** the firms subject to the FCA Conduct of Business Sourcebook
- **Know** the activities which are subject to the FCA Conduct of Business Sourcebook including Eligible Counterparty Business and transactions between regulated market participants
- **Know** the impact of location on firms/activities of the application of the FCA Conduct of Business Sourcebook: permanent place of business in UK
- **Know** the provisions of the FCA Conduct of Business Sourcebook regarding electronic media (Glossary definitions of 'durable medium' and 'website conditions')
- **Know** the recording of voice conversations and electronic communications requirements

Accepting customers

- **Understand** client status
    - The application of the rules on client classification
    - Definition of client
    - Retail client, professional client and eligible counterparty
    - When a person is acting as agent for another person
    - The rule on categorising elective professional clients
    - The rule on elective eligible counterparties
    - Providing clients with a higher level of protection
    - The requirement to provide notifications of client categorisation
- **Know** the requirement for firms to provide client agreements, when a client agreement is required to be signed and when it is acceptable to be provided to clients
- **Know** the rules, guidance and evidential provisions regarding reliance on others

Communicating with clients, including financial promotions

- **Know** the application of the rules on communication to clients and on fair, clear and not misleading communications
- **Know** the purpose and application of the financial promotion rules and the relationship with Principles for Businesses 6 and 7
- **Know** the application of the financial promotion rules and firms' responsibilities for appointed representatives
- **Know** the types of communication addressed by COBS 4 including the methods of communication
- **Know** the main exemptions to the financial promotion rules and the existence of the Financial Promotions Order
- **Know** the rules on approving and communicating financial promotions and compliance with the financial promotions rules

Advising and selling

- **Understand** the purpose and application of the 'suitability' rules; the rule on identifying client needs and advising; and the rules on churning and switching
- **Understand** the application and purpose of the rules on non-advised sales
- **Understand** the obligations for assessing appropriateness
- **Know** the circumstances in which it is not necessary to assess appropriateness

Dealing and managing

- **Know** the application of the rules on dealing and managing
- **Understand** the application and purpose of the principles and rules on conflict of interest; the rules on identifying conflicts and types of conflicts; the rules on recording and disclosure of conflicts
- **Know** the rule requiring a conflicts policy and the contents of the policy
- **Understand** the rule on managing conflicts of interest and how to manage conflicts of interest to ensure the fair treatment of clients including: information barriers such as 'Chinese walls'; reporting lines; remuneration structures; segregation of duties; policy of independence
- **Know** the rules on managing conflict in connection with investment research and research recommendations
- **Know** the application of the inducements rules and the use of dealing commission, including what benefits can be supplied/obtained under such agreements
- **Understand** the requirements of providing best execution
- **Understand** the requirements for an order execution policy, its disclosure, the requirements for consent and review
- **Understand** the rules on following specific instructions from a client
- **Understand** the rules on monitoring the effectiveness of execution arrangements and policy; demonstrating compliance with the execution policy; and the duties of portfolio managers and receivers and transmitters to act in a client's best interest
- **Understand** the rule on client order handling and the conditions to be satisfied when carrying out client orders
- **Understand** the rules on aggregation and allocation of orders and the rules on aggregation and allocation of transactions for own account
- **Know** the rules on client limit orders – the obligation to make unexecuted client limit orders public
- **Understand** the purpose and application of the personal account dealing rule and the restrictions on personal account dealing
- **Know** the arrangements required to comply with the personal account dealing rules including the notification requirements, and exceptions regarding personal account dealing
- **Know** the general client reporting and occasional reporting requirements
- **Know** the rules on periodic reporting to professional clients, the exceptions to the requirements and the record keeping requirements

Client assets

- **Understand** the purpose of the client money and custody rules in CASS, including the requirement for segregation and that it is held in trust
- **Know** the requirements for reconciling client assets and client money including the timing and identification of discrepancies
- **Know** the exemptions from the requirements of the CASS rules

1 COBS: Application and General Provisions

Learning objectives

Know the firms subject to the FCA Conduct of Business Sourcebook

Know the activities which are subject to the FCA Conduct of Business Sourcebook including Eligible Counterparty Business and transactions between regulated market participants

Know the impact of location on firms/activities of the application of the FCA Conduct of Business Sourcebook: permanent place of business in UK

1.1 COBS

The FCA includes various rules in a large section of its Handbook called the **Conduct of Business Sourcebook**. This Sourcebook sometimes is referred to by the abbreviation '**COBS**'.

1.2 General application rule

The **general application rule** is that COBS applies to an authorised **firm** in respect of the following activities when carried out from one of its (or its **appointed representative's**) **UK** establishments.

- Accepting deposits
- Designated investment business
- Long-term life insurance business

Many rules (except the financial promotion rules) only apply when the firm is undertaking **designated investment business** with customers.

The term '**designated investment business**' has a narrower meaning than the concept of '**regulated activities**' by excluding activities relating to deposits, funeral plans, mortgages, pure protection policies and general insurance contracts. Following the implementation of MiFID, operating a **multilateral trading facility (MTF)** is designated investment business.

There are **modifications** to the general application rule. Only some of the COBS rules apply to **eligible counterparty business** which is MiFID or equivalent third country (that is, **non-EEA**) business. The term 'eligible counterparty' is explained later in this chapter. The following COBS rules **do not** apply to such business.

- Conduct of business obligations, except 'Agent as client' and 'Reliance on others' rules
- Communicating with clients (including financial promotions rules)
- Rules on information about the firm and its services and remuneration
- Client agreements
- Appropriateness rules (for non-advised sales)
- Best execution, client order handling and use of dealing commission
- Labelling of non-independent research
- Information about designated investments
- Reporting information to clients

1.3 Further general provisions

The **territorial scope** of COBS is modified to ensure compatibility with European law: this is called the '**EEA territorial scope rule**'. One of the effects of the EEA territorial scope rule is to override the application of COBS to the overseas establishments of EEA firms in a number of cases, including circumstances covered by MiFID, the Distance Marketing Directive or the Electronic Commerce Directive.

4: FCA CONDUCT OF BUSINESS AND CLIENT ASSETS SOURCEBOOKS

In some circumstances, the rules on financial promotions and other communications will apply to communications made by UK firms to persons located outside the United Kingdom and will not apply to communications made to persons inside the United Kingdom by EEA firms.

For a UK **MiFID investment firm**, COBS rules within the scope of MiFID generally apply to its MiFID business carried on from a **UK branch or establishment**. COBS also applies to EEA MiFID investment firms carrying out business from a UK establishment. However, certain provisions (on investment research, non-independent research and on personal transactions) apply on a '**Home State**' **basis**: those rules will apply to all establishments in the EEA for the UK firm, and will not apply to a non-UK EEA firm.

COBS provisions on **client limit orders** do not apply to transactions between the operator of a MTF and its members, for MiFID or equivalent third country business. Members or participants in a **regulated market** do not have to apply client limit orders rules to each other, again for MiFID or equivalent third country business. However, in both cases, these rules must be applied if the members are executing orders on behalf of **clients**.

1.4 Communications by electronic media

> **Learning objective**
>
> **Know** the provisions of the FCA Conduct of Business Sourcebook regarding electronic media (Glossary definitions of 'durable medium' and 'website conditions')

Where a rule requires a notice to be delivered in writing, a firm may comply using **electronic media**. The COBS rules often specify that communication must be in a **durable medium**.

Durable medium means:

- Paper, or
- Any instrument (eg an e-mail message) which enables the recipient to store information addressed personally to him, in a way accessible for future reference for a period of time adequate for the purposes of the information, and which allows the unchanged reproduction of the information stored. This will include the recipient's computer hard drive or other storage devices on which the electronic mail is stored, but not internet web sites unless they fulfil the criteria in this definition.

Some communications are allowed to be delivered either in a durable medium or via a web site, where the **web site conditions** are satisfied.

The **web site conditions** are specified as follows:

1. The provision of the information in that medium must be appropriate to the context in which the business between the firm and the client is, or is to be, carried on (ie there is evidence that the client has regular access to the internet, such as the provision by the client of an e-mail address).
2. The client must specifically consent to the provision of that information in that form.
3. The client must be notified electronically of the address of the web site, and the place on the web site where the information may be accessed.
4. The information must be up-to-date.
5. The information must be accessible continuously by means of that web site for such period of time as the client may reasonably need to inspect it.

1.5 Recording voice communications

Learning objective: **Know** the recording of voice conversations and electronic communications requirements

Firms are required to record telephone conversations and electronic communications, which includes fax, e-mail and instant messaging communications.

The requirement to make recordings applies to activities relating to client orders on prescribed markets, when the business is carried out from the UK. It does not apply to corporate finance business or corporate treasury functions.

Firms are required to record and retain copies of all relevant conversations made on **mobile telephones** where the equipment is **provided to individuals by firms**. Firms must take 'reasonable steps' to ensure that such conversations do not take place on individuals' private telephones, as a firm cannot record these for reasons of privacy.

Records must be kept for at least six months and must be in a form that cannot be manipulated or altered and be readily accessible by the regulator.

2 Accepting Customers

Learning objective: **Understand** client status: The application of the rules on client classification; Definition of client; Retail client, professional client and eligible counterparty; When a person is acting as agent for another person; The rule on categorising elective professional clients; The rule on elective eligible counterparties; Providing clients with a higher level of protection; The requirement to provide notifications of client categorisation

2.1 Levels of protection

Within any cost-effective regulatory system, protection provided ought to be **proportionate** to the need for protection. This is because there is not only a cost element to protection but also an inverse relationship with freedom. It is desirable that those who do not require high protection are given more freedom to trade without the restrictions that the rules inevitably bring.

The level of protection can be linked with the **size** and **financial awareness** of **clients**. Larger or more financially aware clients should generally need less protective regulation. While this would ideally be a continuous process, gradually moving from full protection to no protection, in practical terms this would be an impossibility. A system of categorising clients can help determine that the level of regulatory protection is appropriate to the client.

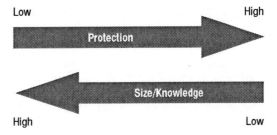

2.2 Client categories

The terms used to classify clients have changed following the implementation of **MiFID** and the introduction of the new COBS.

4: FCA CONDUCT OF BUSINESS AND CLIENT ASSETS SOURCEBOOKS

Firms (unless they are providing only the special level of **basic advice** on **stakeholder products**) are obliged to classify all clients who are undertaking **designated investment business,** before doing such business.

MiFID has created three client categories:

- **Eligible counterparties** – who are either *per se* or **elective** eligible counterparties
- **Professional clients** – who are either *per se* or **elective** professional clients
- **Retail clients**

We saw earlier that a **customer** is a client who is not an eligible counterparty. The scheme of categorisation is summarised in the following diagram.

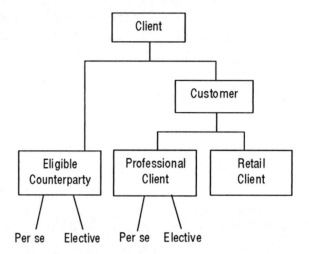

As we shall explain later, as well as setting up criteria to classify clients into these categories, MiFID provides for clients to **change** their initial classification, on request.

2.2.1 Clients

A **client** is a person to whom an authorised **firm** provides a service in the course of carrying on a **regulated activity** or, in the case of MiFID or equivalent third country business, a person to whom a firm provides an **ancillary service**.

2.2.2 Retail clients

Retail clients are defined as those clients who are not professional clients or eligible counterparties.

2.2.3 Professional clients

Some undertakings are automatically recognised as **professional clients**. Accordingly, these entities may be referred to as *per se* professional clients. (An **undertaking** is a company, partnership or unincorporated association.)

Clients who are *per se* **professional clients** are as follows.

- Entities that **require authorisation or regulation** to operate in the financial markets, including: credit institutions, investment firms, other financial institutions, insurance companies, collective investment schemes and pension funds and their management companies, commodity and commodity derivatives dealers, 'local' derivatives dealing firms, and other institutional investors

- In relation to **MiFID** business, **large undertakings** – meaning one that meets two of the following size requirements:
    - €20,000,000 balance sheet total
    - €40,000,000 net turnover
    - €2,000,000 own funds

- For non-**MiFID** business, **large undertakings**, meaning those which:

    (a) Have called-up share capital or net assets of at least £5,000,000 or equivalent (now or at any time in the last two years), **or**

    (b) Meet (or its holding companies or subsidiaries meet) two of the three following size tests:
    - €12,500,000 Balance sheet total
    - €25,000,000 Net turnover
    - 250 average Number of employees in the year

    Trustees of pension schemes with at least 50 members now or in the last two years and assets of at least £10 million, and **trustees of a trust** with assets of at least £10m and **partnerships** or **unincorporated associations** with net assets of at least £5m, are also deemed to be large undertakings for non-MiFID business and so are *per se* **professional clients** for such business.

- Central banks, international institutions, and national and regional government bodies
- Institutional investors whose main activity is to invest in financial instruments

Retail clients can request to **opt up** to be treated as professional clients, for example in order to gain more product freedom or lower charges. These opted up clients are referred to as **'elective' professional clients**. Although broadly similar to an 'expert' private customer under previous COB rules, the qualifying criteria for a retail client to become an 'elective' professional client are more detailed under MiFID.

A firm may treat a retail client as an **elective professional client** if the following tests are met.

- **Qualitative test**. The firm assesses adequately the client's **expertise, experience** and **knowledge** and thereby gains reasonable assurance that, for the transactions or services envisaged, the client is capable of making his own investment decisions and understanding the risks involved.

- **Quantitative test**. In the case of **MiFID** or equivalent third country business, at least **two** of the following three criteria must apply:
    - The client has carried out at least ten 'significant' transactions per quarter on the relevant market, over the last four quarters
    - The client's portfolio, including cash deposits, exceeds €500,000
    - The client has knowledge of the transactions envisaged from at least one year's professional work in the financial sector

Additionally, to opt up to professional client status:

- The client must agree in writing to be treated as a professional client
- The firm must give written warning of the protections and compensation rights which may be lost
- The client must state in writing, separately from the contract, that it is aware of the consequences of losing protections

It is the responsibility of the professional client to keep the firm informed about changes (eg in portfolio size or company size) which could affect their categorisation.

COBS states that an elective professional client should not be presumed to have market knowledge and experience comparable to a *per se* professional client.

2.2.4 Eligible counterparties

In relation to MiFID or equivalent third country business, a client can only be an eligible counterparty in relation to eligible counterparty business.

Eligible counterparty business covers the following relatively simple types of business:

- Dealing on own account
- Execution of orders on behalf of clients
- Reception and transmission of orders
- Any ancillary service directly related to a service or activity above

It would not cover a firm asking for advice, nor fund management services.

The following, and their non-EEA equivalents, are *per se* **eligible counterparties** (ie they are automatically recognised as eligible counterparties).

- Insurance companies, investment firms and credit institutions
- UCITS collective investment schemes, and their management companies
- Pension funds, and their management companies
- Other EEA-authorised financial institutions
- National governments, central banks and supranational organisations

A firm may treat an undertaking as an **elective eligible counterparty** if the client:

- Is a *per se* professional client (unless it is such by virtue of being an institutional investor), or
- Is an elective professional client and requests the categorisation, but only in respect of the transactions and services for which it counts as a professional client, and
- In the case of MiFID or equivalent third country business, provides 'express confirmation' of their agreement (which may be for a specific transaction or may be general) to be treated as an eligible counterparty

If the prospective counterparty is established in another EEA State, for MiFID business the firm should defer to the status determined by the law of that other State.

2.3 Providing a higher level of protection to clients

Firms must allow **professional clients** and **eligible counterparties** to re-categorise in order to get more protection. Such clients are themselves responsible for asking for higher protection if they deem themselves to be **unable** to assess properly or manage the risks involved.

Either on the firm's own initiative or following a client request or written agreement:

- A *per se* **eligible counterparty** may be re-categorised as a **professional client** or **retail client**
- A *per se* **professional client** may be re-categorised as a **retail client**

The **higher level of protection** may be provided through re-categorisation:

- On a general basis
- Trade by trade
- In respect of specified rules
- In respect of particular services, transactions, transaction types or product types

The client should (of course) be notified of a re-categorisation.

Firms must have written internal policies and procedures to categorise clients.

2.4 Agent as client

One area that has proved complicated in the past is where a firm is dealing with an **agent**. For example, suppose that a solicitor is acting for his client and approaches a firm to sell bonds on his client's behalf. Clearly, it is important that the firm establish whether it owes duties to the solicitor or to the solicitor's client.

The agent is the client of the firm, unless an agreement in writing treats the other person as the client.

The relevant COBS rule applies to designated investment business and ancillary services. The rule states that the firm may treat the agent as its client if the agent is another authorised firm or an overseas financial services institution **or** if the agent is another person, provided that the arrangement is not to avoid duties which the firm would otherwise owe to the agent's clients.

An agreement may however be made, in writing, to treat the other person (in the above example, the solicitor's client) as the firm's client.

2.5 Client agreements

> **Learning objective**
>
> **Know** the requirement for firms to provide client agreements, when a client agreement is required to be signed and when it is acceptable to be provided to clients

If a firm carries on **designated investment business**, other than advising on investments, for a **new retail client**, the firm must enter into a **basic agreement** with the client. Thus, for example, there should be a client agreement when discretionary investment management services are provided. Although little guidance is given in the rules as to the contents, the agreement will set out the essential rights and obligations of the firm, and must be in writing – on paper or other durable medium. For a **professional client**, there is no requirement for an agreement, although most firms will wish there to be one.

In good time, normally **before** the client is bound by any agreement relating to designated investment business or ancillary services, the firm must provide to the retail client – either in a durable medium or on a web site, if the web site conditions are satisfied:

- The terms of the agreement
- Information about **the firm and its services** (see below), including information on communications, conflicts of interest and authorised status

The agreement and information may be provided **immediately after** the client is bound by the agreement if the agreement was concluded using a means of distance communication (eg telephone).

Relevant material changes to the information provided must be notified to the client in **good time**.

2.6 Reliance on others

> **Learning objective**
>
> **Know** the rules, guidance and evidential provisions regarding reliance on others

Suppose that a firm (**F1**) carrying out MiFID or equivalent third country business receives an instruction from an investment firm (**F2**) to perform an investment or ancillary service on behalf of a client (**C**).

F1 may rely on:

- Information about the client **C** which firm **F2** provides
- Recommendations about the service provided to **C** by **F2**

F2 remains responsible for the completeness and accuracy of information provided and the appropriateness of its advice.

More generally, a firm is taken to be in **compliance with COBS** rules which require it to obtain information, if it can show it was **reasonable** for it to rely on information provided by others in writing. It is reasonable to rely on written information provided by another where that person is **competent** and **not connected** with the firm.

This rule links with Principle 2 *Skill, Care and Diligence.* Note that this rule has no impact on the requirements laid down in the Money Laundering Regulations, which require a firm to identify its clients for money laundering purposes.

3 COMMUNICATIONS WITH CLIENTS

Learning objectives

Know the application of the rules on communication to clients

Know the purpose and application of the financial promotion rules and the relationship with Principles for Businesses 6 and 7

Know the application of the financial promotion rules and firms' responsibilities for appointed representatives

Know the types of communication addressed by COBS 4 including the methods of communication

3.1 Financial promotions and communications

A **financial promotion** is an **invitation** or **inducement** to engage in investment activity. The term therefore describes most forms and methods of marketing financial services. It covers traditional advertising, most web site content, telephone sales campaigns and face-to-face meetings. The term is extended to cover **marketing communications** by MiFID.

The Treasury has indicated that **purely factual communications** would not amount to an invitation or inducement and so would not be financial promotions.

The purpose of regulation in this area is to create a regime where the quality of financial promotions is scrutinised by an authorised firm who must then comply with lengthy rules to ensure that their promotions are **clear, fair and not misleading** (Principle 7) and that customers are treated **fairly** (Principle 6).

3.2 Application of the financial promotions rules

The **financial promotions rules** within COBS apply to a firm:

- Communicating with **retail and professional clients** in relation to **designated investment business**

- **Communicating** or **approving** a **financial promotion** (with some exceptions in respect of: credit promotions, non-investment insurance contracts, unregulated collective investment schemes (UCIS), home purchase plans and home reversion schemes – rules for financial promotions in various home finance areas are covered in MCOB)

Firms must also apply the rules to promotions issued by their **appointed representatives**.

3.3 Territorial scope

For financial promotions, the **general application rule** applies. This indicates that the rules apply to a firm in respect of designated investment business carried out from an establishment maintained by the firm or its appointed representative in the UK. Additionally, in general the rules apply to firms carrying on business with a client in the UK from an establishment overseas.

The financial promotions rules also apply to:

- Promotions communicated to a person in the UK
- Cold (unsolicited) calling to someone outside the UK, if the call is from within the UK or is in respect of UK business

3.4 Fair, clear and not misleading

> **Learning objective**
>
> **Know** the application of the rule on fair, clear and not misleading communications

A firm must ensure that:

A communication or financial promotion is **fair, clear and not misleading**, as is **appropriate** and **proportionate** considering the means of communication and the information to be conveyed.

This rule applies to financial promotions communicated by the firm **except**:

- Communications directed at professional clients or eligible counterparties (ie 'non-retail')
- Excluded communications (see below), and
- Third party prospectuses in respect of designated investment business

Additionally, Part 7 Financial Services Act 2012 creates a criminal offence relating to certain **misleading statements and impressions**.

The **fair, clear and not misleading rule** is specifically interpreted in COBS as it applies to financial promotions in some aspects, as follows.

- If a product or service places a client's capital at risk, this should be made clear
- Any yield figure quoted should give a balanced impression of both short-term and long-term prospects for the investment
- Sufficient information must be provided to explain any complex charging arrangements, taking into account recipients' needs
- The full name of the regulator should be stated, and any non-regulated aspects made clear
- A fair, clear and not misleading impression should be given of the producer for any packaged products* or stakeholder products not produced by the firm

* A **packaged product** is defined as one of the following:

- A life policy
- A unit in a regulated collective investment scheme
- An interest in an investment trust savings scheme
- A stakeholder pension scheme
- A personal pension scheme

whether or not (in the case of the first three types listed above) the product is held within an ISA or a Child Trust Fund (CTF) and whether or not the packaged product is also a stakeholder product.

3.5 Exceptions to the financial promotions rules

> **Learning objective**
> **Know** the main exemptions to the financial promotion rules and the existence of the Financial Promotions Order

As indicated earlier, the **financial promotions rules** in COBS do **not apply** to promotions of qualifying credit, home purchase plans, home reversion schemes, non-investment insurance contracts, and certain unregulated collective investment schemes whose promotions firms may not communicate or approve.

Except in regard to disclosure of compensation arrangements, the COBS rules on communications (including financial promotions) do **not** apply when a firm communicates with an **eligible counterparty**.

The financial promotions rules also do **not** apply to incoming communications in relation to **MiFID business** of an investment firm **from another EEA State** that are, in its Home State, regulated under MiFID.

3.6 Excluded communications

A firm may rely on one or more of the following aspects which make a communication into an **excluded communication** for the purposes of the rules.

- A financial promotion that would benefit from an exemption in the Financial Promotion Order (see below) if it were communicated by an unauthorised person, or which originates outside the UK and has no effect in the UK
- A financial promotion from outside the UK that would be exempt under Articles 30, 31, 32 or 33 of the Financial Promotion Order (Overseas communicators) if the office from which the financial promotion is communicated were a separate unauthorised person
- A financial promotion that is subject to, or exempted from, the Takeover Code or to the requirements relating to takeovers or related operations in another EEA State
- A personal quotation or illustration form
- A '**one-off**' **financial promotion** that is not a cold call. The following conditions indicate that the promotion is a 'one-off', but they need not necessarily be present for a promotion to be considered as 'one-off'.
    - The financial promotion is communicated only to one recipient or only to one group of recipients in the expectation that they would engage in any investment activity jointly
    - The identity of the product or service to which the financial promotion relates has been determined having regard to the particular circumstances of the recipient
    - The financial promotion is not part of an organised marketing campaign

3.7 FCA financial promotions power

As we saw earlier, the FCA has a new **power** under the Financial Services Act 2012 (s137R FSMA 2000, as amended) **to ban misleading financial promotions**.

- The regulator will be able to give a **direction** to firms requiring them immediately to withdraw or to modify promotions which it deems to be misleading, and to publish such decisions.
- The firm will be able to make **representations** to the FCA to challenge the Authority's decision. The FCA may then decide to amend or revoke its decision, or it may confirm its original decision. After having given the firm the opportunity to challenge the decision, the FCA can publish: (1) Its

direction, (2) A copy of the promotion, and (3) The regulator's reasons for banning it. The FCA may publish details even if it has decided to revoke its decision.

3.8 Financial Promotions Order (FPO)

Section 21 FSMA 2000 makes it criminal for someone to undertake a financial promotion, ie **invite or induce** another to engage in **investment activity**, **in the course of business**, unless they are either:

- An **authorised firm** (ie, the firm **issuing the financial promotion**), or
- The content of the communication is **approved** by an authorised firm

Note the following points on the words above.

- The terms '**invite**' or '**induce**' have their natural meaning. This means there must be a degree of incitement rather than the simple provision of factual information. Every case must be judged in the light of the circumstances to determine whether it attempts to invite or induce.
- The term '**investment activity**' generally relates to controlled investments which is a similar definition to specified investments. This means that the financial promotions rules do not only cover designated investment business.
- The term '**in the course of business**' again has its natural meaning and requires some commercial element to the promotion.

Contravention of section 21 is punishable by up to **two** years in jail and an **unlimited** fine in the Crown Court, or six months' imprisonment and a statutory maximum of £5,000 in the Magistrates' Court.

There are various exemptions from s21 set out in the **Financial Promotions Order (FPO), as amended**, including the following significant ones.

- **Generic promotions** – for example, promotions for investment trusts, in general
- **Investment professionals** – communications to an authorised or exempt person
- Communications with **overseas recipients** – ie outside the UK
- **Deposits and insurance** – for which COBS has very limited application
- **One-off communications** – see above
- **Certified high net worth individuals** – with a net income of £100,000 or more, or net assets, excluding their principal property, of £250,000 or more
- **Certified sophisticated investors** – who are knowledgeable in a particular stock

The effect of being an **exemption** is that the promotion would **not** need to be issued or approved by an authorised firm. It would not therefore have to comply with the detailed financial promotion rules.

Note also the **excluded communications** above.

3.9 Approving financial promotions

> **Learning objective**
> **Know** the rules on approving and communicating financial promotions and compliance with the financial promotions rules

The rules in **SYSC** require that a firm which communicates with a client regarding designated investment business, or communicates or approves a financial promotion, puts in place **systems and controls** or **policies and procedures** in order to comply with the COBS rules.

As we have seen, **FSMA 2000** prohibits an unauthorised person from communicating a financial promotion, unless either an exemption applies or the financial promotion is approved by an authorised firm. Approval of a financial promotion by an **authorised firm** enables it to be communicated by an **unauthorised firm**.

A firm **approving** a financial promotion must confirm that it **complies** with the **financial promotion rules**. The firm must withdraw its approval, and notify anyone it knows to be relying on its approval, if it becomes aware that it no longer complies with the financial promotion rules.

A **real-time financial promotion**, that is one made during a personal visit, telephone conversation or other **interactive dialogue**, cannot be approved.

Approval given by the firm may be '**limited**', eg limited to communication to **professional clients** or **eligible counterparties**.

In communicating a financial promotion, a firm is permitted to **rely on another firm's confirmation of compliance** with the financial promotions rules. The firm must take reasonable care to ensure that the promotion is only communicated to types of recipients for whom it was intended.

4 ADVISING AND SELLING

Learning Objective: **Understand** the purpose and application of the 'suitability' rules; the rule on identifying client needs and advising

4.1 Assessing suitability

Suitability rules apply when a firm makes a **personal recommendation** in relation to a **designated investment** (but special rules apply if the firm is giving basic scripted advice for stakeholder products), and when a firm is **managing investments**.

For non-MiFID business, these rules apply to business with **retail clients**. For MiFID business, they apply to both **retail and professional clients**. When making personal recommendations or managing investments for **professional clients**, in the course of MiFID or equivalent third country business, a firm is entitled to assume that the client has the necessary experience and knowledge, in relation to products and services for which the professional client is so classified.

The rules put obligations on the firm to **assess suitability**: the firm must take reasonable steps to ensure that, in respect of designated investments, a personal recommendation or a decision to trade is **suitable for its client**.

To meet this obligation, the firm must **obtain necessary information** regarding the client's:

- **Knowledge and experience** in the relevant investment field (including: types of investment or service with which the client is familiar; transactions experience; level of education and profession or former profession; understanding of risks)

- **Investment objectives** (including: length of time he wishes to hold the investment; risk preferences; risk profile; purposes of the investment)

- **Financial situation** (including: extent and source of regular income; assets including liquid assets; investments and real property; regular financial commitments) (Is he able to bear any investment risks, consistent with his investment objectives?)

The firm is entitled to **rely on information provided by the client**, unless it is aware that the information is out-of-date, inaccurate or incomplete.

A **transaction** may be **unsuitable** for a client because of:

- The risks of the designated investments involved
- The type of transaction
- The characteristics of the order
- The frequency of trading
- It resulting in an unsuitable portfolio (in the case of **managing investments**)

4.2 Suitability report requirement

A firm must provide a **suitability report** to a retail client if the firm makes a personal recommendation and the client:

- Buys or sells shares/units in a regulated collective investment scheme
- Buys or sells shares through an investment trust savings scheme or investment trust ISA
- Makes or changes contributions to a personal or stakeholder pension scheme
- Elects to make income withdrawals from a short-term annuity
- Enters into a pension transfer or pension opt-out

A suitability report is required for all personal recommendations in relation to **life policies**.

A suitability report is **not** required:

- If the firm acts as investment manager and recommends a regulated collective investment scheme
- If a non-EEA resident is not in the UK when acknowledging consent to the proposal form
- For small life policies (premiums not >£50 p.a.) recommended by friendly societies
- For recommendations to increase regular premiums on an existing contract
- For recommendations to invest further single contributions to an existing packaged product

The suitability report must generally be provided to the client **as soon as possible after the transaction is effected**. For personal or stakeholder pension schemes requiring notification of cancellation rights, the report must be provided no later than 14 days after the contract is concluded.

The suitability report must, at least:

- Specify the client's **demands and needs**
- Explain the firm's **recommendation** that the transaction is suitable, having regard to information provided by the client
- Explain any possible **disadvantages** of the transaction to the client

The firm should give details appropriate to the **complexity** of the transaction.

For **income withdrawals** from a **short-term annuity**, the explanation of possible disadvantages should include **risk factors** involved in income withdrawals or purchase of a short-term annuity.

4.3 Non-advised sales

Learning Objectives	**Understand** the application and purpose of the rules on non-advised sales **Understand** the obligations for assessing appropriateness **Know** the circumstances in which it is not necessary to assess appropriateness

4.3.1 Appropriateness rules

The central aim of the appropriateness rules – which were introduced under **MiFID** – is to prevent complex products from being sold on an **execution only** basis (that is, without advice) to **retail clients** who do not have the experience and/or the knowledge to understand the risks of such products.

The **appropriateness** rules apply to a firm providing **MiFID investment services, other than** making a personal recommendation and managing investments ('non-advised sales'). (As we have seen, the **suitability** rules apply where there is a personal recommendation.) The rules thus apply to '**execution only**' services which are available in the UK, where transactions are undertaken at the initiative of the customer without advice having been given.

Additionally, for both MiFID and non-MiFID business, the appropriateness rules apply to arranging or dealing in **derivatives** or **warrants** for a **retail client**, when in response to a **direct offer financial promotion**. The FCA Handbook Glossary defines **derivatives** as comprising **contracts for differences (CfDs), futures and options**.

Except for the case of direct offer business, the appropriateness test is not required for non-MiFID business: therefore, it does not apply to non-MiFID products such as insurance policies, deposits (including structured deposits) and pension plans.

To **assess appropriateness**, the firm must ask the client to provide information on his knowledge and experience in the relevant investment field, to enable the assessment to be made.

The firm will then:

- Determine whether the client has the necessary **experience and knowledge** to understand the **risks** involved in the product/service (including the following aspects: nature and extent of service with which client is familiar; complexity; risks involved; extent of client's transactions in designated investments; level of client's education and profession or former profession)
- Be entitled to assume that a **professional client** has such experience and knowledge, for products/services for which it is classified as 'professional'

Unless it knows the information from the client to be out-of-date, inaccurate or incomplete, the firm may rely on it. Where reasonable, a firm may infer knowledge from experience. One firm may rely on another MiFID firm's assessment of appropriateness, in line with the general rule on reliance on other investment firms.

The firm may seek to increase the client's level of understanding by providing appropriate information to the client.

If the firm is satisfied about the client's experience and knowledge, there is **no duty to communicate** this to the client. If the firm concludes that the product or service is **not appropriate** to the client, it must **warn** the client. The warning may be in a standardised format.

If the client provides insufficient information, the firm must **warn** the client that such a decision will not allow the firm to determine whether the service or product is appropriate for him. Again, the warning may be in a standardised format.

If a client who has received a warning asks the firm to go ahead with the transaction, it is for the firm to consider whether to do so 'having regard to the circumstances'.

Records relating to appropriateness must be kept for at least **five years**.

4.3.2 When is an assessment of appropriateness not needed?

A firm does **not** need to seek information from the client or assess appropriateness if:

- The service consists only of execution and receiving / transmitting client orders for particular **financial instruments** (see below), provided at the initiative of the client
- The client has been informed clearly that in providing this service the firm is not required to assess suitability and that therefore he does not receive protection from the suitability rules, and
- The firm complies with obligations regarding conflicts of interest

The particular **financial instruments** are:

- Shares on a regulated or equivalent third country market
- Money market instruments, bonds and other forms of securitised debt (excluding bonds and securitised debt which embed a derivative)
- Units in a UCITS scheme
- Other non-complex financial instruments (among the requirements to qualify as 'non-complex' are that they cannot lead the investor to lose more than they invested, adequate information is freely available, there is a market for them with prices made available independently of the issuer, and they do not give rise to cash settlement in the way that many derivatives do)

For a **course of dealings** in a specific type of product or service, the firm does not have to make a new assessment for each transaction.

If a client has engaged in a **course of dealings before 1 November 2007** (the MiFID implementation date), he is presumed to have the necessary experience and knowledge to understand the risks involved.

A firm need not assess appropriateness if it is receiving or transmitting an order for which it has assessed **suitability** under the COBS suitability rules (covered above). Also, a firm may not need to assess appropriateness if it is able to rely on a recommendation made by a **different investment firm**.

5 DEALING AND MANAGING

5.1 Application of rules

> **Learning Objective**
> **Know** the application of the rules on dealing and managing

COBS includes rules on **dealing and managing**. These rules (except for the rules on personal account dealing – see below) apply to **MiFID business** carried out by a **MiFID investment firm**, and to equivalent third country business.

The provisions on **personal account dealing** apply to designated investment business carried on from a UK establishment. They also apply to passported activities carried on by a UK MiFID investment firm from a branch in another EEA State, but not to the UK branch of an EEA MiFID investment firm in relation to its MiFID business.

5.2 Conflicts of interest

> **Learning Objectives**
>
> **Understand** the application and purpose of the principles and rules on conflict of interest; the rules on identifying conflicts and types of conflicts; the rules on recording and disclosure of conflicts
>
> **Know** the rule requiring a conflicts policy and the contents of the policy
>
> **Understand** the rule on managing conflicts of interest and how to manage conflicts of interest to ensure the fair treatment of clients including: information barriers such as 'Chinese walls'; reporting lines; remuneration structures; segregation of duties; policy of independence

5.2.1 Principle 8

Inevitably, authorised firms, particularly where they act in dual capacity (both broker and dealing for the firm itself), are faced with **conflicts** between the firm and customers or between one customer and another.

Principle 8 of the *Principles for Businesses* states: 'A firm must manage conflicts of interest fairly, both between itself and its customers and between a customer and another client'.

Principle 8 thus requires that authorised firms should seek to ensure that when **conflicts of interest** do arise, the firm **manages** the conflicts to ensure that customers are treated **fairly**.

One way in which a potential conflict of interest may be dealt with is, of course, by declining to act for the client.

5.2.2 SYSC 10

SYSC 10 applies to common platform firms carrying on regulated activities and ancillary activities or providing MiFID ancillary services, where a service is provided, to any category of client.

The firm must take all **reasonable steps** to **identify conflicts of interest** between the firm, its managers, employees and appointed representatives or tied agents, or between clients, which may arise in providing a service.

The firm must take into account, as a minimum, likely financial gains, or avoidance of losses, at the expense of a client, interests in the outcome of a service which are different from the client's interest, financial incentives to favour some clients or groups of client, and whether the firm carries on the same business as the client, or receives inducements in the form of monies, goods and services other than the standard commission or fee for that service.

Regularly updated records must be kept of where conflicts of interest have or may arise.

The firm must maintain and operate effective **organisational and administrative arrangements** to prevent conflicts of interest from giving rise to material risk of damage to clients' interests.

Where conflicts are not preventable by any other means, as a last resort the firm must **disclose** them to clients – in a durable medium, in sufficient detail for the client to take an informed decision – before undertaking business.

Firms should aim to **identify** and **manage** conflicts under a **comprehensive conflicts of interest policy**. That firms actively manage conflicts is important: 'over-reliance on disclosure' without adequate consideration of how to manage conflicts is not permitted.

5.2.3 Conflicts policy

Common platform firms must maintain an effective **conflicts of interest policy**, in **writing** and appropriate to the size and type of firm and its business.

The conflicts of interest policy must:

- Identify circumstances constituting or potentially giving rise to conflicts materially affecting clients
- Specify procedures and measures to manage the conflicts

The procedures and measures must be designed to ensure that activities are carried on with an appropriate **level of independence** (this part of the procedures is often called a **policy of independence**).

As and where necessary, procedures must be included:

- To **prevent and control exchange of information** between persons involved (see below on **Chinese walls**)
- To **supervise persons separately** (ie using appropriate **reporting lines**)
- To remove **links in remuneration** producing possible conflicts
- To prevent exercise of **inappropriate influence**
- To **prevent and control simultaneous and sequential involvement** of persons in separate services or activities (eg through **segregation of duties** between different personnel)

In drawing up its conflicts policy, the firm must pay **special attention** to the following **activities** (in particular, where persons perform a combination of activities): investment research and advice, proprietary trading, portfolio management and corporate finance business, including underwriting or selling in an offer of securities, and advising on mergers and acquisitions.

If managing an **offering of securities**, the firm might wish to consider agreeing:

- Relevant aspects of the offering process with the corporate finance client at an early stage
- Allocation and pricing objectives with the corporate finance client, inviting the client to participate actively in the allocation process, making the initial recommendation for allocation to retail clients as a single block and not on a named basis and disclosing to the issuer the allocations actually made

5.2.4 'Chinese walls'

Chinese walls are administrative and physical barriers and other internal arrangements, designed to contain **sensitive information**. Most commonly, they are used around the corporate finance departments of firms that often have confidential, sometimes inside, information.

Chinese walls **do not have to be used** by firms, but if they are, this rule becomes relevant.

Where a firm establishes and maintains a Chinese wall, it allows the persons on one side of the wall, eg corporate finance, to withhold information from persons on the other side of the wall, eg equity research.

A firm will not be guilty of **market abuse** (s118A(5)(a)) or be liable to a lawsuit under **s150 FSMA 2000** where the failure arises from the operation of a Chinese wall.

An example of the effect of the Chinese wall rule is as follows. Suppose that a corporate finance department has plans for a company that will change the value of the company's shares. The equity salesman on the other side of the 'wall' should have no knowledge of these plans; consequently his inability to pass this knowledge on to clients is not seen as a failure of his duty to them.

5.3 Investment research and conflicts of interest

Learning Objective	**Know** the rules on managing conflict in connection with investment research and research recommendations

5.3.1 Introduction

There have been concerns that analysts have been encouraged to write favourable research on companies in order to attract lucrative investment banking work. There have also been concerns about firms' employees recommending particular securities while privately trading contrary to the recommendation.

COBS rules on investment research apply to MiFID business carried on by a MiFID investment firm. Rules on disclosure of research recommendations apply to all firms.

5.3.2 Investment research

The rules cover investment research which is intended or likely to be disseminated to clients or to the public.

Firms must ensure that its measures for **managing conflicts of interest** cover the **financial analysts** who produce its investment research, and any other relevant staff.

The firm's arrangements must ensure that:

- The financial analysts and other staff involved do not undertake personal transactions or trade on behalf of other persons, including the firm (unless they are acting as a market maker in good faith or executing an unsolicited client order), in financial instruments to which unpublished investment research relates, until the **recipients** of the research have had a **reasonable opportunity** to act on it

- In other circumstances, personal transactions by financial analysts and other staff in financial instruments related to investment research they are producing which is **contrary to current recommendations** must only occur in **exceptional circumstances** and with **prior approval** of the firm's legal or compliance function

- The firm and its staff must not **accept inducements** from those with a material interest in the subject matter of investment research, and they must not **promise issuers favourable research coverage**

- Issuers and persons other than financial analysts must not be allowed to **review pre-publication drafts** of investment research for any purpose **other than to verify compliance** with the firm's legal obligations, if the draft includes a recommendation or a target price

There is an exemption from these rules where a firm distributes investment research **produced by a third party** which is not in the firm's group, provided that the firm does not alter the recommendations and does not present the research as produced by the firm. The firm is required to verify that the independent producer of the research has equivalent arrangements in place to avoid conflicts of interest.

5.3.3 Non-independent research

Investment research is research which is described as investment research or in similar terms, or is otherwise presented as an objective or independent explanation of the matters contained in the recommendation. Research not meeting this requirement falls within the definition of **non-independent research**.

Non-independent research must:

- Be clearly identified as a **marketing communication**
- Contain a clear and prominent statement that it does not follow the requirements of independent research and is not subject to prohibitions on dealing ahead of dissemination of research

Financial promotions rules apply to non-independent research as if it were a marketing communication.

Firms must take **reasonable care** to ensure that research recommendations are fairly presented, and to disclose its interests or indicate conflicts of interest.

Situations where conflicts can arise include:

- Employees trading in financial instruments which they know the firm has or intends to publish non-independent research about, before clients have had a reasonable opportunity to act on the research (other than where the firm is acting as a market maker in good faith, or in the execution of an unsolicited client order)
- Non-independent research intended first for internal use and for later publication to clients

5.3.4 Research recommendations: required disclosures

The **identity** (name, job title, name of firm, competent authority) of the person responsible for the research should be disclosed clearly and prominently.

The research should meet certain **general standards**, for example to ensure that facts are distinguished from interpretations or opinions. Projections should be labelled as such. Reliable sources should be used, and any doubts about reliability clearly indicated. The substance of the recommendations should be possible to be substantiated by the regulator on request.

Additionally, the firm must take reasonable care to disclose its own interests and any conflicts of interest, and to ensure **fair presentation**, broadly covering the following aspects.

- Indication of material sources, including the issuer (if appropriate)
- Disclosure of whether the recommendation was communicated to the issuer and then amended
- Summary of valuation basis or methodology
- Explanation of the meaning of any recommendation (eg, 'buy', 'sell', 'hold')
- Risk warning if appropriate
- Planned frequency of updates
- Date of release of research, and date and time of prices mentioned
- Details of change over any previous recommendation in the last year

Firms must make **disclosures** in research recommendations broadly covering the following areas.

- All **relationships and circumstances** (including those of affiliated companies) that may reasonably be expected to impair the objectivity of the recommendation (especially, financial interests in any relevant investment, and a conflict of interest regarding the issuer)

- Whether employees involved have **remuneration** tied to investment banking transactions

- **Shareholdings** held by the firm (or an affiliated company) of over 5% of the share capital of the issuer

- **Shareholdings** held by the issuer of over 5% of the share capital of the firm (or an affiliated company)

- Other **significant financial interests**

- Statements about the **role of the firm** as market maker, lead manager of previous offers of the issuer in the last year, provider of investment banking services

- Statements about **arrangements** to prevent and avoid conflicts of interest, prices and dates at which employees involved acquired shares

- **Data** on the proportions of the firm's **recommendations** in different categories (eg 'buy', 'sell', 'hold'), on a quarterly basis, with the proportions of relevant investments issued by issuers who were investment banking clients of the firm during the last year

- Identification of a **third party** who produced the research, if applicable, describing also any alteration of third party recommendations and ensuring that any summary of third party research is fair, clear and not misleading

For shorter recommendations, firms can make reference to many of the relevant disclosures, for example by providing a **web site link**.

5.4 Inducements

> **Learning Objective**
>
> **Know** the application of the inducements rules and the use of dealing commission, including what benefits can be supplied/obtained under such agreements

A firm must **not** pay or accept any fee or commission, or provide or receive any non-monetary benefit, in relation to designated investment business, or an ancillary service in the case of MiFID or equivalent third country business, other than:

- Fees, commissions and non-monetary benefits paid or provided to or by the client or a person on their behalf
- Fees, commissions and non-monetary benefits paid or provided to or by a third party or a person acting on their behalf, if the firm's duty to act in the best interests of the client is not impaired, and (for MiFID and equivalent business, and where there is a personal recommendation of a packaged product, but not for 'basic advice') clear, comprehensive, accurate, understandable disclosure (except of 'reasonable non-monetary benefits', listed later) is made to the client before the service is provided. (Thus, the rule on inducements does not apply to discloseable commissions.)

This rule supplements Principles 1 and 6 of the *Principles for Businesses*. It deals with the delicate area of inducements and seeks to ensure that firms do not conduct business under arrangements that may give rise to conflicts of interest.

Inducements could mean anything from gifts to entertainment to bribery. The rules provide a test to help judge whether or not something is acceptable.

Where **commissions** must be disclosed in relation to packaged products the firm should not pay commission based on the volume of business transacted, nor should there be agreements to indemnify payment of commission which might give an additional financial benefit to the recipient if the commission becomes repayable. If the firm selling packaged products enters into an agreement under which it receives commission more than that disclosed to the client, rules on disclosure of charges and inducements are likely to have been breached.

In the case of retail business, there are rules to prevent a product provider from taking a **holding of capital** in the firm or providing **credit** to an advisory firm unless stringent terms are met, including a condition requiring the holding or credit to be on commercial terms. This is to prevent conflicts of interest and bias, eg through channelling of business.

In relation to retail investment products (RIPs), the following are broadly deemed to be **reasonable non-monetary benefits**.

- Gifts, hospitality and promotional prizes of reasonable value, given by product provider to the firm
- Assistance in promotion of a firm's RIPs
- Generic product literature which enhances client service, with costs borne by the recipient firm
- Generic technical information
- Training facilities
- Reasonable travel and accommodation expenses, eg to meetings or training

If a product provider makes benefits available to one firm but not another, this is more likely to impair compliance with the **client's best interests rule**. Most firms deliver against the inducements requirements by drafting detailed '**gifts policies**' (although the rule does **not** explicitly require firms to have a gifts policy). These contain internal rules regarding disclosure, limits and clearance procedures for gifts.

5.5 Use of dealing commission

The practice of **using dealing commission** (previously called **soft commission**) dates back many years. The practice developed from brokers effectively **rebating** part of the commission paid by large fund management clients, to be used to cover the costs of services such as equity research. The effect was to reduce the 'real' commission paid for the execution of the trade. It is deemed necessary to control these arrangements to ensure that customers who ultimately pay the commissions, namely the fund managers' clients, are protected from abuse.

The rules on the use of dealing commission aim to ensure that an investment manager's arrangements, in relation to dealing commissions spent on acquiring services in addition to execution, are transparent and demonstrate accountability to customers so that customers are treated fairly.

The rules therefore help to ensure firms comply with Principle 1 (Integrity), Principle 6 (Customers' Interests) and Principle 8 (Conflicts of Interest).

The rules on the use of dealing commission apply to investment managers when executing customer orders through a broker or another person in shares or other investments which relate to shares, eg warrants, hybrids (ADRs and options) and rights to, or interests in, investments relating to shares.

When the investment manager passes on the broker's or other person's charges (whether commission or otherwise) to its customers and in return arranges to receive goods or services **the rules require the investment manager to be satisfied that the goods or services**:

- Relate to the execution of trades, or
- Comprise the provision of research

This is subject to a clause that the goods or services will reasonably assist the investment manager in the provision of services to its customers and do not impair compliance with the duty of the investment manager to act in the best interests of its customers.

For **goods or services** relating to the execution of trades, the regulator has confirmed that post-trade analytics, eg performance measurement, is not going to be an acceptable use of dealing commission. Where the goods or services relate to research, the investment manager will have to be satisfied that the research:

- Is capable of **adding value** to the investment or trading decisions by providing **new insights** that inform the investment manager when making such decisions about its customers' portfolios
- In whatever form its output takes, represents **original thought**, in the critical and careful consideration and assessment of new and existing facts, and does not merely repeat or repackage what has been presented before
- Has **intellectual rigour** and does not merely state what is commonplace or self-evident, and
- Involves analysis or manipulation of data to reach **meaningful conclusions**

Examples of goods or services that relate to the execution of trades or the provision of research that are **not** going to be **acceptable** to the regulator include the following.

- Services relating to the valuation or performance measurement of portfolios
- Computer hardware
- Dedicated telephone lines and other connectivity services
- Seminar fees
- Subscriptions for publications
- Travel, accommodation or entertainment costs
- Order and execution management systems
- Office administration computer software, eg for word processing or accounting

- Membership fees to professional associations
- Purchase or rental of standard office equipment or ancillary facilities
- Employees' salaries
- Direct money payments
- Publicly available information
- Custody services relating to designated investments belonging to, or managed for, customers

Investment managers must make **adequate prior disclosure** to customers about receipt of goods and services that relate to the execution of trades or the provision of research. This should form part of the summary form disclosure under the rule on inducements. **Periodic disclosures** made on an annual basis are recommended.

5.6 Best execution

> **Learning Objective**: **Understand** the requirements of providing best execution

The basic COBS rule of **best execution** applies to business with both retail and professional clients and is stated as follows:

> 'A firm must take all reasonable steps to obtain, when executing orders, the best possible result for its clients taking into account the execution factors.'

The execution factors are price, costs, speed, likelihood of execution and settlement, size, nature or any other consideration relevant to the execution of an order.

In determining the relative importance of the execution factors, firms must take into account the following **best execution criteria**:

- The client, including categorisation as retail or professional
- The client order
- The financial instruments
- The execution venues

The '**best possible result**' must be determined in terms of **total consideration** – taking into account any costs, including the firm's own commissions in the case of competing execution venues, and not just quoted prices. (However, the firm is not expected to compare the result with that of clients of other firms.) Commissions structure must not discriminate between execution venues.

When a firm is **dealing on own account with clients**, this is considered to be execution of client orders, and is therefore subject to the best execution rule.

If a firm provides a best quote to a client, it is acceptable for the quote to be executed after the client accepts it, provided the quote is not manifestly out of date.

The obligation to obtain best execution needs to be interpreted according to the particular type of financial instrument involved, but the rule applies to **all types of financial instrument**.

5.7 Order execution policy

Learning Objectives	**Understand** the requirements for an order execution policy, its disclosure, the requirements for consent and review
	Understand the rules on following specific instructions from a client
	Understand the rules on monitoring the effectiveness of execution arrangements and policy; demonstrating compliance with the execution policy; and the duties of portfolio managers and receivers and transmitters to act in a client's best interest

5.7.1 Policy requirements

The firm must establish and implement an **order execution policy**, and it must monitor its effectiveness regularly.

The policy must include, for each class of financial instruments, information on different execution venues used by the firm, and the factors affecting choice of execution venue.

The firm should choose venues that enable it to obtain on a consistent basis the best possible result for execution of client orders. For each client order, the firm should apply its execution policy with a view to achieving the best possible result for the client.

If orders may be executed outside a regulated market or MTF, this must be disclosed, and clients must give prior express consent.

A firm must be able to demonstrate to clients, on request, that it has followed its execution policy.

5.7.2 Client consent and clients' specific instructions

The firm must provide a **retail client** with details on its execution policy before providing the service, covering the relative importance the firm assigns to execution factors, a list of execution venues on which the firm relies, and a clear and prominent warning that **specific instructions** by the client could prevent the firm from following its execution policy steps fully.

If the client gives **specific instructions**, the firm has met its best execution obligation if it obtains the best result in following those instructions. The firm should not induce a client to give such instructions, if they could prevent best execution from being obtained. However, the firm may invite the client to choose between execution venues.

The firm must obtain the **prior consent** of clients to its execution policy, and the policy must be **reviewed annually** and whenever there is a material change in the firm's ability to achieve the best possible result consistently from execution venues.

5.7.3 Portfolio management and order reception and transmission services

Firms who act as **portfolio managers** must comply with the **clients' best interests rule** when placing orders with other entities. Firms who provide a service of **receiving and transmitting orders** must do the same when transmitting orders to other entities for execution. Such firms must:

- Take all reasonable steps to obtain the best possible result for clients
- Establish and maintain a policy to enable it to do so, and monitor its effectiveness
- Provide appropriate information to clients on the policy
- Review the policy annually or whenever there is a material change affecting the firm's ability to continue to obtain the best possible result for clients

5.8 Client order handling

> **Learning Objective**
> Understand the rule on client order handling and the conditions to be satisfied when carrying out client orders

The rules on **client order handling** apply for both retail and professional clients. The general rule is that firms must implement procedures and arrangements which provide for the prompt, fair and expeditious execution of client orders, relative to other orders or the trading interests of the firm.

These procedures and arrangements must allow for the execution of otherwise comparable orders in accordance with the time of their reception by the firm.

When carrying out **client orders**, firms must:

- Ensure that orders are promptly and accurately recorded and allocated
- Carry out otherwise comparable orders sequentially and promptly, unless this is impracticable or not in clients' interests
- Inform a retail client about any material difficulty in carrying out orders promptly, on becoming aware of it

Where it is not practicable to treat orders sequentially, eg because they are received by different media, they should not be treated as 'otherwise comparable'.

Firms must not allow the **misuse of information** relating to pending client orders. Any use of such information to deal on own account should be considered a misuse of the information.

When overseeing or arranging **settlement**, a firm must take reasonable steps to ensure that instruments or funds due are delivered to the client account promptly and correctly.

5.9 Aggregation and allocation

> **Learning Objective**
> Understand the rules on aggregation and allocation of orders and the rules on aggregation and allocation of transactions for own account

Aggregation (grouping together) of client orders with other client orders or a transaction for own account is not permitted unless:

- It is unlikely to work to the disadvantage to any of the clients
- It is disclosed to each client that the effect of aggregation may work to their disadvantage
- An **order allocation policy** is established and implemented, covering the fair allocation of aggregated orders, including how the volume and price of orders determines allocations, and the treatment of partial executions

The order allocation policy must prevent reallocation of transactions on own account executed in combination with client orders, in a way that is detrimental to the client (eg if unfair precedence is given to the firm or another person).

If a firm aggregates a client order with a transaction on own account, and the aggregated order is partially executed, it must allocate the related trades **to the client in priority** to the firm, although if it can demonstrate that the aggregation enabled advantageous terms to be obtained, it may allocate the transaction proportionally.

5.10 Client limit orders

Learning Objective: **Know** the rules on client limit orders – the obligation to make unexecuted client limit orders public

A **limit order** specifies a limit at or below which a client agrees to buy, or at or above which a client agrees to sell.

Unless the client expressly instructs otherwise, a firm has an obligation to make unexecuted client limit orders (for shares on a regulated market) public, to facilitate the earliest possible execution. The order may be made public by transmitting it to a regulated market or MTF.

For **eligible counterparties**, this obligation to disclose applies only where the counterparty is explicitly sending a limit order to a firm for its execution.

The obligation to make public will not apply to a limit order that is **large** in scale compared with the **normal market size** for the share.

5.11 Personal account dealing

Learning Objectives: **Understand** the purpose and application of the personal account dealing rule and the restrictions on personal account dealing

Know the arrangements required to comply with the personal account dealing rules including the notification requirements, and exceptions regarding personal account dealing

Personal account dealing relates to trades undertaken by the staff of a regulated business for themselves, or by those providing outsourced services for the firm. Such trades can create **conflicts of interest** between staff and customers. As a matter of good practice, a firm's policy on personal account dealing should generally be extended to immediate family members.

A firm conducting **designated investment business** must establish, implement and maintain adequate **arrangements** aimed at preventing employees who are involved in activities where a conflict of interest could occur, or who has access to inside information, from:

- Entering into a transaction which is prohibited under the **Market Abuse Directive**, or which involves misuse or improper disclosure of confidential information, or conflicts with an obligation of the firm to a customer under the regulatory system

- Except in the course of his job, advising or procuring anyone else to enter into such a transaction

- Except in the course of his job, disclosing any information or opinion to another person if the person disclosing it should know that, as a result, the other person would be likely to enter into such a transaction or advise or procure another to enter into such a transaction

The **firm's arrangements** under these provisions must be designed to ensure that:

- All relevant persons (staff involved) are aware of the personal dealing restrictions

- The firm is informed promptly of any personal transaction

- A service provider to whom activities are outsourced maintain a record of personal transactions and provides it to the firm promptly on request

- A record is kept of personal transactions notified to the firm or identified by it, including any related authorisation or prohibition

The rule on personal account dealing is **disapplied** for personal transactions:

- Under a discretionary portfolio management service where there has been no prior communication between the portfolio manager and the person for whom the transaction is executed
- In UCITS collective undertakings (eg OEICs and unit trusts) where the person is not involved in its management
- In life policies
- For successive personal transactions where there were prior instructions in force, and to the termination of the instruction provided that no financial instruments are sold at the same time

5.12 Churning and switching

> **Learning Objective**
> **Understand** the rules on churning and switching

Churning and switching are similar wrongs. They involve the cynical **overtrading** of customer accounts for the purpose of generating commission. This clearly contravenes the **client's best interests rule**.

Churning or switching will often be difficult to isolate, unless blatant. Much depends upon the market conditions prevailing at the time of dealing.

The **COBS rules** on churning and switching state that:

- A series of transactions that are each suitable when viewed in isolation may be unsuitable if the recommendations or the decisions to trade are made with a frequency that is not in the best interests of the client
- A firm should have regard to the client's agreed investment strategy in determining the frequency of transactions. This would include, for example, the need to switch within or between packaged products

6 REPORTING TO CLIENTS

> **Learning Objectives**
> **Know** the general client reporting and occasional reporting requirements
> **Know** the rules on periodic reporting to professional clients, the exceptions to the requirements and the record keeping requirements

6.1 Reporting executions

For **MiFID** and equivalent third country business, a firm must ensure that clients receive **adequate reports** on the services provided to it by the firm and their costs.

A firm must provide promptly in a durable medium the **essential information** on **execution of orders** to clients in the course of **designated investment business**, when it is not managing the investments. The information may be sent to an agent of the client, nominated by the client in writing. Confirmations (also called 'contract notes') must be provided by the next business day (T + 1) for retail clients.

Firms must supply information about the **status of a client's order** on request.

For **series of orders** to buy units or shares in a collective undertaking (such as a **regular savings plan**), after the initial report, further reports must be provided at least at six-monthly intervals.

Where an order is executed in tranches, the firm may supply the price for each tranche or an average price. The price for each tranche must be made available on the request of a retail client.

For business that is not MiFID or equivalent third country business, confirmations need **not** be supplied if:

- The **client has agreed** not to receive them (with informed written consent, in the case of retail clients), or
- The designated investment is a **life policy** or a **personal pension scheme** (other than a SIPP), or
- The designated investment is held in a **Child Trust Fund** and the information is contained in the annual statement

6.2 Periodic reporting

A firm **managing investments** on behalf of a professional client must provide a periodic statement to the client in a durable medium, unless such a statement is provided by another person.

For a **retail client**, the **periodic statement** should be provided once every **six months**, except that:

- In the case of a leveraged portfolio, it should be provided at least **once a month**.
- It should be provided every **three months** if the client requests it (the firm must inform clients of this right).
- If the retail client elects to receive information on a transaction-by-transaction basis and there are no transactions in derivatives or similar instruments giving rise to a cash settlement, the periodic statement must be supplied at least once every **twelve months**.

A firm managing investments (or operating a retail client account that includes an uncovered open position in a contingent liability transaction – involving a potential liability in excess of the cost) must report to the client any **losses** exceeding any **predetermined threshold** agreed with the client.

Periodic statements for **contingent liability transactions** may include information on the **collateral value** and **option account valuations** in respect of each option written by the client in the portfolio at the end of the relevant period.

For **non-MiFID business**, a firm need not provide a periodic statement to a client habitually resident outside the UK if the client does not wish to receive it.

6.3 Record-keeping

Copies of **confirmations** and **periodic reports** must be **kept** for at least **five years** from the date of despatch, for MiFID and equivalent third country business, and for at least **three years** in other cases.

7 CLIENT ASSETS RULES

> **Learning Objective**
>
> **Understand** the purpose of the client money and custody rules in CASS, including the requirement for segregation and that it is held in trust

7.1 Overview

The rules in this section link to Principle for Businesses 10 *Clients' Assets*. The rules aim to restrict the commingling of client's and firm's assets and minimise the risk of client's investments being used by the firm without the client's agreement or contrary to the client's wishes, or being treated as the firm's assets

4: FCA CONDUCT OF BUSINESS AND CLIENT ASSETS SOURCEBOOKS

in the event of its **insolvency**. The focus therefore is on two main issues, namely custody of investments, and client money.

The client assets rules have a broader coverage than the rules contained in COBS, the Conduct of Business Sourcebook, in that they afford protection not only to retail and professional clients, but also to **eligible counterparties**.

As we have seen earlier in this Study Text, under MiFID, client assets are regulated by the firm's **Home State**. Therefore, for example, if a French firm is **passporting** into the UK, it will adhere to French client assets rules.

The implementation of MiFID has resulted in more onerous requirements on firms in respect of custody of client assets and client money. In January 2009 revisions to CASS, non-MiFID and MiFID rules were largely harmonised.

- Except in the case of credit institutions, firms may not use client funds for their own account in any circumstances.
- Sub-custodians and depositaries must be selected in accordance with specified rules.
- There are rules specifying that client funds be held with particular types of bank and (if the client does not object) certain money market funds meeting specified criteria.
- One of the most significant impacts of MiFID implementation on the existing client money regime is that MiFID firms may not allow professional clients to 'opt-out' of the client money rules, for MiFID business.
- A firm holding money for an affiliated company in respect of MiFID business must treat the affiliated company as any other client of the firm.

Firms face **risks** that should be managed and mitigated, including **settlement risk** – the risk that arises from a transaction not being completed properly or on time – and **counterparty risk** – the risk that the counterparty to a transaction may default. Firms must introduce adequate organisational arrangements to minimise the risk of the loss of or diminution of clients' safe custody assets and client money as a result of misuse, fraud, poor administration, inadequate record-keeping or negligence.

The **Client Assets (CASS)** section of the FCA Handbook includes custody rules for **custody** and **client money** which apply to a firm which holds financial instruments belonging to a client.

7.2 Holding client assets

Firms sometimes hold investments on behalf of clients in physical form, eg bearer bonds, or may be responsible for the assets but not physically holding them as they are held elsewhere, eg with another custodian or via CREST.

Firms which hold financial instruments belonging to clients must make arrangements to **safeguard clients' ownership rights**, especially in the event of the firm's insolvency. Firms are not permitted to use financial instruments which are held for clients **for their own account** unless they have the express consent of the client.

The firm must have **adequate organisational arrangements** to minimise risk of loss or diminution of clients' financial instruments or of rights over them resulting from misuse, fraud, poor administration, inadequate record-keeping or other negligence.

As far as practicable, the firm must effect registration or recording of legal title to financial instruments, normally in the name of:

- The client, or
- A nominee company

For nominee companies controlled by the firm, the firm has the same level of responsibility to the client regarding custody of the assets.

In the case of **overseas financial instruments**, where it is in the client's best interests, the instruments may be held by:

- Any other party, in which case the client must be notified in writing
- The firm, subject to written consent (if a retail client) or notification of the client (for professional clients)

7.3 Requirement to protect client money

A firm must make adequate arrangements to safeguard clients' rights over **client money** the firm holds, and to prevent the use of client money for the firm's own account. Client money rules apply to money held on behalf of clients in connection with MiFID business and designated investment business. Thus, the rules do not apply to funds held in a bank deposit account.

As with financial instruments, the firm must have **adequate organisational arrangements** to minimise risk of loss or diminution of clients' money or of rights over such money resulting from misuse, fraud, poor administration, inadequate record-keeping or other negligence.

If a firm leaves some of its own money in a client money account, this will be referred to as a '**pollution of trust**' and, if the firm fails, the liquidator will be able to seize all the money held in the client account for the general creditors of the firm.

A firm should undertake adequate **due diligence** before placing any client assets or client money with third parties. The due diligence should amount to more than simply checking the credit rating of the institution. Appropriate due diligence might assess a bank's market reputation, assess legal requirements or market practices, and consider risk diversification as well as credit ratings on an ongoing basis, The due diligence review carried out should be documented.

Client money must be deposited with:

- A central bank
- An EEA credit institution
- A bank authorised in a third country, or
- A qualifying money market fund

Following the collapse of Lehman Brothers, it transpired that 50% of Lehman Brothers International (Europe)'s had placed 50% of its client money with a group bank that became insolvent. In response to this, a rule was made with effect from 1 June 2011, applying to firms a **20% maximum limit on intra-group client money deposits** in client bank accounts.

7.4 Statutory trust

Section 139(1) FSMA 2000 provides for creation of a fiduciary relationship (a **statutory trust**) between the firm and its client, under which client money is in the legal ownership of the firm but remains in the beneficial ownership of the client. In the event of failure of the firm, costs relating to the distribution of client money may have to be borne by the trust.

A firm receives and holds client money as trustee (or as agent, in Scotland):

- For the clients concerned, and then
- For paying costs in distributing client money, and only after all valid claims have been met,
- For the firm itself

7.5 Internal reconciliation of financial instruments held for clients

> **Learning Objective**
> **Know** the requirements for reconciling client assets and client money including the timing and identification of discrepancies

Carrying out **internal reconciliations** of **financial instruments held (as 'safe custody assets') for clients** is part of discharging the firm's obligations to have accurate records and accounts, robust governance arrangements and procedures to counter the risk of financial crime.

To ensure accuracy of accounts and records, firms should perform such internal reconciliations as often as is necessary, and as soon as reasonably practicable after the date to which the reconciliation relates.

Possible reconciliation methods include the '**total count method**', which requires that all of the safe custody assets be counted and reconciled as at the same date.

A firm using an **alternative reconciliation method** (for example the '**rolling stock method**'):

- Must first send a written confirmation to the regulator from the firm's **auditor** that the firm has in place systems and controls which are adequate to enable it to use the method effectively
- Must ensure that all of a particular safe custody asset are counted and reconciled **as at the same date** and that all safe custody assets are counted and reconciled during a period of **six months**

7.6 Financial instruments: reconciliations with external records

The firm should ensure that any **third party** holding clients' **financial instruments** provides regular statements.

To ensure accuracy of its records, the firm must carry out regular reconciliations between its own records and those of such third parties:

- As regularly as is necessary, and
- As soon as possible after the date to which the reconciliation relates

The person, who may be an employee of the firm, carrying out the reconciliation should, whenever possible, be someone who is independent of the process of producing and maintaining the records (this type of control being called **segregation of duties**).

If a firm has not complied with the reconciliation requirements 'in any material respect', then it must inform the regulator without delay.

7.7 Financial instruments: reconciliation discrepancies

Any **discrepancies** revealed in the reconciliations – including items recorded in a suspense or error account – must be corrected promptly.

Any unreconciled shortfall must be made good, if there are reasonable grounds for concluding that the firm is responsible. If the firm concludes that someone else is responsible, steps should be taken to resolve the position with that other person.

If a firm has not made good an unreconciled shortfall 'in any material respect', then it must inform the regulator without delay.

7.8 Client money: reconciliations with external records

Broadly, if a firm holds money that belongs to someone else, then that money is client money.

As with financial instruments, to ensure accuracy of its records, the firm must carry out regular reconciliations between its own client money records and those of third parties, such as a bank, holding **client money**:

- As regularly as is necessary, and
- As soon as possible after the date to which the reconciliation relates

In determining the **frequency** of reconciliations, the firm should **consider relevant risks**, such as the nature, volume and complexity of the business, and where the client money is held.

The regulator recommends that reconciliations should compare and identify discrepancies between:

- The balance of each **client bank account** as recorded by the firm, *and* the balance shown on the bank's statement, and
- The balance as shown in the firm's records, currency by currency, on each **client transaction account** – for **contingent liability investments**, which includes certain derivatives, spot forex trades, spread bets and CfDs – *and* the balance shown in the third party's records.

Any **approved collateral** held must be included in the reconciliation.

7.9 Client money: reconciliation discrepancies

The **reason** for any **discrepancy** must be identified, unless it arises solely from timing differences between a third party's accounting systems and those of the firm.

Any **shortfall** must be paid into (or any **excess** withdrawn from) the client bank account by the close of business on the day the reconciliation is performed.

If a firm cannot resolve a difference between its internal records and those of a third party holding client money, the firm must pay its own money into a relevant account to make up any difference, until the matter is resolved.

As with financial instruments held, if a firm has not complied with the reconciliation requirements in respect of client money 'in any material respect', then it must inform the regulator without delay.

7.10 Exemptions from CASS rules

Learning Objective

Know the exemptions from the requirements of the CASS rules

There are some circumstances in which the client money rules described here do not apply.

CASS does not apply to:

- An investment company with variable capital (ICVC) (ie an OEIC)
- An incoming EEA firm other than an insurer, with respect to its passported activities
- A UCITS qualifier (a firm qualified to operate UCITS collective investment schemes)
- An authorised professional firm with respect to its non-mainstream regulated activities
- The Society of Lloyd's

Custody rules do not apply where a client transfers full ownership of a safe custody asset to a firm for the purpose of securing or otherwise covering present or future, actual, contingent or prospective obligations.

7.10.1 Credit institutions

The client money rules do not apply to **Banking Consolidation Directive (BCD) credit institutions** in respect of deposits. Institutions whose business is to receive deposits from the public are credit institutions.

7.10.2 Coins held for intrinsic value

Client money rules do not apply to **coins** held on behalf of a client, if the firm and client have agreed that the money is to be held by the firm for the **intrinsic value** of the **metal** in the coin.

7.10.3 DVP transactions

Short-term money arising through **delivery versus payment (DVP) transactions** through a commercial settlement system will not normally need not be treated as client money. **DVP** is a form of securities trading in which payment and transfer of the subject security occur simultaneously.

7.10.4 Discharge of fiduciary duty

Money **ceases to be client money** if it is paid:

- To the client or his authorised representative, or into a bank account of the client
- To the firm itself, when it is due and payable to the firm, or is an excess in the client bank account
- To a third party, on the client's instruction, unless it is transferred to a third party to effect a transaction – for example, a payment to an intermediate broker as initial or variation margin on behalf of a client who has a position in derivatives. In these circumstances, the firm remains responsible for that client's equity balance held at the intermediate broker until the contract is terminated and all of that client's positions at that broker closed

7.11 CASS Resolution Pack

The regulator introduced rules taking effect on **1 October 2012** that require firms to which either or both of CASS 6 (custody rules) and CASS 7 (client money rules) applies to maintain and be able to retrieve a **CASS Resolution Pack (CASS RP)**. The CASS RP contains documents and records that would help an insolvency practitioner to return client assets more quickly following an investment firm failure.

Rules require firms to ensure that CASS RP documents can be retrieved within 48 hours and that material inaccuracies in the content of certain CASS RP documents are corrected within five business days of the inaccuracy arising.

Following the collapse of both Lehman Brothers International (Europe) (LBIE) and (in 2011) MF Global UK Limited, the introduction of the CASS RP is one step towards ensuring the speedier return of client assets.

7.12 Client Asset Unit

The regulator has established a **Client Asset Unit**, within its Markets Division of the Conduct Business Unit, to focus specialist resources on CASS issues.

The Unit was created to provide confidence in the ability of the UK regulatory regime to deliver adequate protection of client money and safe custody assets (client assets), which is a critical component for a successful financial services industry.

The regulator has stated that it relies on the quality of the protections afforded by the client assets regime because they help to ensure that clients' assets and money are safe in the event of firms failing and exiting the market. Weaknesses in firms' client asset systems and controls can cause serious financial detriment to customers and counterparties, as well as reputational damage to the regulator and to UK markets.

The **Client Asset Unit's mission** is to help minimise the risk of financial loss from control failings and mitigate the damaging effects of such potential failures on consumers, firms and the regulator.

Relevant **desirable regulatory outcomes** are as follows.

- Clients to be confident that their assets are being held by firms with robust client asset controls as well as strong risk management
- Clients to be assured that their client assets are safe and will be returned within a reasonable timeframe in the event of firm failure
- The UK market to be regarded as a safe place to conduct business and encourage market entrants

8 COBS Summary

The following table summarises some of the important rules in the **Conduct of Business Sourcebook (COBS)** that are covered in this chapter. Reference numbers given are to the relevant COBS section. While you need to have **knowledge** of the rules, you should also be able to **apply** the rules to the various scenarios the examiner may present.

COBS rule	Main points	Exceptions	Further notes
Application of COBS (1)	COBS applies to authorised firms and its appointed representative business, for: ■ Accepting deposits ■ Designated investment business (DIB) ■ Long-term life insurance COBS MiFID rules apply to MiFID business of UK MiFID investment firms carried on from UK branch or establishment.	Some rules apply only to DIB. Only some rules apply to MiFID eligible counterparty (ECP) business.	Deposits, mortgages, protection policies and general insurance are not DIB.
Recording communications (11.8)	Keep recordings for six months of 'phone and electronic communications.	Corporate finance and treasury.	
Client categorisation (3)	Firms must classify clients before doing investment business, as one of: ■ ECPs: *per se* or elective ■ Professional clients: *per se* or elective ■ Retail clients	Basic advice on stakeholder products.	A client is a person receiving a service that is a regulated activity, or a MiFID ancillary service.
Categorising elective professional clients (3.5.3 – 3.5.9)	A retail client can be treated as a professional client, subject to qualitative test (expertise, experience and knowledge) and quantitative test (on portfolio size, transaction volume or work experience).		Written agreement is required, including written warnings about reduced protections.
Elective ECPs (3.6.4 – 3.6.6)	Professional clients providing 'express confirmation' can be treated as ECPs.		
Re-categorisation, for more protection (3.7)	Professional clients and ECPs must be given more protection, either generally or for specific business, if they ask for it.		

COBS rule	Main points	Exceptions	Further notes
Agent as client (2.4.2)	Firms may treat agents who are authorised or overseas financial firms as clients.	Duties owed to agent's clients must not be avoided.	
Reliance on others (2.4.4)	Firms may rely on another competent firm's information about a client, and its recommendations.	Rule has no impact on anti-money laundering requirements.	
Communication with clients and financial promotions (FPs) (4)	FP: an invitation or inducement to engage in investment activity, ie most marketing of financial services FP regime aims to ensure FPs are scrutinised by authorised firms, so that customers are treated fairly (PRIN 7). The FCA can ban misleading promotions. The FP rules apply: - To communications with a DIB client - When communicating or approving a FP - For FPs issued by appointed representatives Communications and FPs must be (PRIN 6): - Fair - Clear - Not misleading FPs addressed to clients must generally be identified as such. For DIB with retail clients, communications should generally: - Include name of firm - Be accurate and give a fair and prominent indication of risks, along with potential benefits - Be understandable by an average person from the group likely to receive it - Not disguise, diminish or obscure important items, statements or warnings	FP rules do not apply to: - ECP business, generally - Home-State regulated EEA firms - Qualifying credit promotions, certain home purchase plans - Personal quotations or illustrations - One-off FPs that are not cold calls - Communications exempt under the FP Order, including deposits and insurance, promotions subject to Takeover Code, and promotions to investment professionals, high net worth individuals and sophisticated investors	Part 7 FSA 2012 additionally deems as criminal offences certain misleading statements and impressions
Approving FPs (4.10)	Firm approving an FP must confirm it complies with the FP rules. An approved FP can be communicated by an unauthorised firm. Approval may be limited, eg to professional clients or to ECPs.		Section 21(1) FSMA 2000 requires FPs to be approved by an authorised firm, unless exempt (see earlier). SYSC requires systems and controls or policies and procedures to be in place.

COBS rule	Main points	Exceptions	Further notes
Suitability (9)	Rules apply where personal recommendation given, in relation to DIB, and when managing investments. To ensure that the recommendation or decision to trade is suitable for its client, firm must obtain information (which may come from client) on: - Knowledge and experience in the investment field - Investment objectives, including timescale, risk profile - Financial situation	Non-MiFID business: the rules apply to retail clients. MiFID business: the rules apply to retail and professional clients. Special rules apply to basic advice on stakeholder products. Professional client can be assumed to have knowledge/ experience in their areas.	
Appropriateness (10)	Applies to non-advised services. Firm must assess from information provided by the client his knowledge and experience in the relevant investment field, but does not have to communicate this to the client. Firm may go ahead with transaction if, having been warned that the firm has insufficient information, the client asks the firm to proceed.	Not applicable to ECP business. Professional client can be assumed to have knowledge/ experience in their areas. Appropriateness assessment not required for execution-only services relating to non-complex financial instruments, including listed shares	
Dealing and managing rules: application (11.1)	COBS 11 applies to MiFID business of a MiFID investment firm.	Exception: 11.7 – see below.	
Conflicts of interest (12)	Common platform firms must maintain an effective and appropriate written conflicts of interest policy: - Identifying circumstances leading to conflict - Specifying measures to manage conflict Firms cannot be found guilty under s150 or market abuse provisions, for situations arising from having a Chinese wall.		PRIN 8 states that a firm must manage conflicts of interest fairly.

COBS rule	Main points	Exceptions	Further notes
Investment research and non-independent research (12.1–12.4)	Measures for managing conflicts of interest must cover financial analysts producing investment research, to ensure that: ■ Analysts do not deal in securities before research recipients can ■ Analysts do not generally deal contrary to recommendations without prior approval ■ Inducements are not accepted ■ Issuers are not promised favourable coverage ■ Research is reviewed before publication only to check compliance Non-independent research must be identified as a marketing communication, with a prominent statement that it is not independent research. FP rules apply.	Rules are on 'Home State' basis, and so do not apply to non-UK EEA firms. Research distributed by the firm, but produced by a third party which has conflicts of interest arrangements, is exempt from the rules.	
Inducements (2.3)	To avoid conflicts of interest, paying or accepting inducements is prohibited, other than: ■ What is paid/ provided to/ by client or on their behalf ■ Where duty to act in client's best interests is not impaired (subject to rules on disclosure to the client) ■ Deemed reasonable non-monetary benefits as specified, for packaged products		
Use of dealing commission (11.6)	Where investment managers pass on brokers' charges to customers, goods and services received in return from brokers must: ■ Relate to trade executions, or ■ Comprise provision of appropriate research	Not applicable to ECP business.	
Best execution (11.2)	Firms must take all reasonable steps to get the best possible result (total consideration after costs) for clients when executing orders, depending on type of financial instrument, type of client and execution venue. Firms must have an order execution policy, which will explain factors affecting execution venue choice.	Not applicable to ECP business.	

COBS rule	Main points	Exceptions	Further notes
Client order handling (11.3)	Firms' procedures and arrangements must provide for prompt, fair and expeditious execution of client orders.	Not applicable to ECP business.	
Aggregation and allocation (11.3)	Any aggregation of orders must be unlikely to be disadvantageous to any client, and must be explained to the client. Re-allocation of own account/ client orders must not be to detriment of clients.		
Client limit orders (11.4)	Unexecuted client limit orders must be made public by transmitting to a regulated market, unless client instructs otherwise.	Does not apply between MTF and its members nor between members of a regulated market.	
Personal account dealing (11.7)	Provisions apply to DIB from a UK establishment. Firms' arrangements must avoid market abuse, improper disclosure of information and conflict with obligations to clients.	Rules are on 'Home State' basis, and so do not apply to non-UK EEA firms.	
Churning (investments) and switching (9.3)	Overtrading of client accounts to generate commission contravenes the client's best interests rule and is prohibited.		
Confirmations and statements (16.1–16.3)	Prompt information on order executions must be provided (by the next business day, for retail clients). Investment managers must provide periodic statements.	Not applicable to ECP business. Non-MiFID client may elect not to receive confirmations and (if outside UK) periodic reports. Not applicable to CTFs which provide information annually.	
Record-keeping (Sch 1)	Firms must retain MiFID business records for at least five years. Different limits apply for some non-MiFID business, the general principle being to retain as long as relevant for the purpose.		

Chapter Roundup

- The Conduct of Business Sourcebook (COBS) generally applies to authorised firms engaged in designated investment business carried out from their (or their appointed representatives') UK establishments. Some COB rules do not apply to eligible counterparty business.

- 'Designated investment business' is business involving regulated activities, except mortgages, deposits, pure protection policies, general insurance, Lloyd's business and funeral plans.

- Records of voice communications and electronic communications must be kept for at least six months. A firm may deliver written notices electronically.

- The level of protection given to clients by the regulatory system depends on their classification, with retail clients being protected the most. Professional clients and eligible counterparties may both be either *per se* or elective. Both professional clients and eligible counterparties can re-categorise to get more protection.

- Firms doing designated investment business, except advising, must set out a basic client agreement. Firms must provide to clients appropriate information about the firm and its services.

- It is generally acceptable for a firm to rely on information provided by others if the other firm is competent and not connected with the firm placing the reliance.

- A financial promotion inviting someone to engage in investment activity must be issued by or approved by an authorised firm. Communications must be fair, clear and not misleading.

- Rules on assessing suitability of the recommendation apply when a firm makes a personal recommendation in relation to a designated investment.

- There are obligations to assess 'appropriateness' – based on information about the client's experience and knowledge – for complex instruments, other than when making a personal recommendation or managing investments.

- Firms must seek to ensure fair treatment if there could be a conflict of interest. Common platform firms must maintain an effective conflicts of interest policy. Conflicts of interest policies must cover financial analysts producing investment research.

- Inducements must not be given if they conflict with acting in the best interests of clients. There are controls on the use of dealing commission.

- A firm must in general take all reasonable steps to obtain, when executing orders, the best possible result for its clients. This is the requirement of best execution. There must be arrangements for prompt, fair and expeditious client order handling, and a fair order allocation policy. Unexecuted client limit orders must normally be made public, to facilitate early execution.

- Firms must establish arrangements designed to prevent employees entering into personal transactions which are prohibited forms of market abuse. Staff must be made aware of the personal dealing restrictions.

- Churning and switching are forms of unsuitable overtrading of customer accounts in order to generate commission.

- There are requirements to send out confirmation notes promptly, and periodic statements (valuations) regularly.

- Client assets rules aim to restrict the commingling of client's and firm's assets and to prevent misuse of client's investments by the firm without the client's agreement, or being treated as the firm's assets in the event of the firm's insolvency.

Test Your Knowledge

Check your knowledge of the chapter here, without referring back to the text.

1.	Name the three main categories of client.	▪ ▪ ▪
2.	Name three types of *per se* eligible counterparty.	▪ ▪ ▪
3.	A firm's communications and financial promotions must be '……, ….. and not …'. *Fill in the blanks.*	▪ ▪ ▪
4.	What is the FPO?	
5.	What information will the firm need to obtain from the client to enable it to assess the appropriateness of a product or service to the client?	
6.	What is the name for administrative and physical barriers and other internal arrangements, designed to contain sensitive information?	
7.	What does the rule on best execution require?	
8.	What is the difference between a Confirmation Note and a Periodic Statement?	

4: FCA CONDUCT OF BUSINESS AND CLIENT ASSETS SOURCEBOOKS

| 9. | What is the effect of a statutory trust created under s139(1) FSMA 2000? | |

Test Your Knowledge: Answers

1. Eligible counterparties, professional clients and retail clients.

    (See Section 2.2)

2. Investment firms, national governments and central banks are all examples.

    (See Section 2.2.4)

3. Fair, clear and not misleading.

    (See Section 3.4)

4. The FPO is the Financial Promotions Order. It contains a number of exemptions from s21 FSMA and the rules on financial promotions.

    (See Section 3.8)

5. The firm will need to ask the client for information about his knowledge and experience in the relevant investment field, so that it can assess whether the client understands the risks involved.

    (See Section 4.3)

6. 'Chinese walls'.

    (See Section 5.2.4)

7. The best execution rule requires a firm to take all reasonable steps to obtain, when executing orders, the best possible result for its clients, taking into account the execution factors.

    (See Section 5.6)

8. A Confirmation Note confirms the essential details of each trade and must be sent out within one business of the trade date (within T + 1 for retail clients). A periodic statement gives the value and contents of a portfolio and is normally sent out every six months.

    (See Sections 6.1 & 6.2)

9. Section 139(1) FSMA 2000 provides for creation of a fiduciary relationship (a statutory trust) between the firm and its client, under which client money is in the legal ownership of the firm but remains in the beneficial ownership of the client.

    (See Section 7.4)

Index

Accepted market practices, 82
Administering investments, 50
Agent as client, 129
Aggregation (of orders), 146
American Depository Receipts (ADRs), 52
Ancillary services (MiFID), 111
Anti-Terrorism, Crime and Security Act 2001, 99
Appointed representative, 41
Appropriateness test, 136
Approved persons, 17, 62
Asset Freezing Unit, 95
Assistance (money laundering), 88
Audit plan, 23
Authorisation, 53

Bank of England, 9
Basel Committee on Banking Supervision, 106
Basel II, 106
Basel III, 107
Best execution, 144
Business Model – Threshold Condition, 55
Business to be Conducted in a Prudent Manner – Threshold Condition, 55
Buy-back and Stabilisation Regulation, 84

Capital adequacy, 105
Capital Requirements Directive (CRD), 106
Capital resources requirement, 106
CASS Resolution Pack, 154
Chancellor of the Exchequer, 6
Charities, 42
Chartered Institute for Securities and Investment (CISI), 20
Chinese walls, 139
Churning, 148
Civil standard of proof (market abuse), 83
Client (defined), 15
Client agreements, 129
Client Asset Unit, 154
Client assets rules, 150
Client categorisation, 125
Client limit orders, 147
Client money, 149
Client order handling, 146
Client's best interests rule, 17
Close period, 102

Code of Market Conduct, 83
Code of Practice for Approved Persons, 18
Collective investment schemes, 50, 52
Communications (with clients), 130
Competent employees rule, 64
Competition Commission, 27, 28
Competition objective (FCA), 11
Compliance function, 23, 91
Compliance oversight, 92
Conduct of Business Sourcebook (COBS), 123
Confirmations, 149
Conflicts of interest, 138
Conflicts of interest (investment research), 140
Consolidated List, 95, 100
Consumer protection objective (FCA), 11
Consumer protection strategy, 12
Contingency funding plan, 108
Contingent liability investments, 153
Continuing Professional Development (CPD), 65, 67
Contracts for Difference (CfDs), 53
Contracts of insurance, 49, 52
Control of Misleading Advertising Regulations, 27
Controlled functions, 17, 62
Counterparty risk, 150
Counter-Terrorism Act 2008, 100
Counter-terrorism financing (CTF), 87, 92
Criminal Justice Act 1993, 77, 86
Customer (defined), 15
Customer due diligence (CDD), 96
Customers, 16, 126

Data Protection Act 1998, 103
Data Protection Principles, 104
Davidson, Paul ('The Plumber'), 83
Dealing and managing rules, 137
Dealing as principal, 51
Dealing commission (use of), 143
Dealing in investments, 49
Decision Notice, 43
Decision Procedure and Penalties Manual (DEPP), 44
Delayed disclosure (of inside information), 101
Delivery versus payment (DVP) transactions, 154

INDEX

Department for Business, Innovation and Skills, 79
Deposits, 49, 52
Designated investment business, 123, 126
Designated professional bodies (DPBs), 42
Directions (Handbooks), 30
Directors dealings, 102
Disclosure Rules and Transparency Rules (DTR), 101, 102
Dissemination (market abuse), 82
Distortion (market abuse), 82
Dual regulation, 8, 105
Due diligence defence (market abuse), 84
Durable medium, 124
Duty to report (terrorism), 99

EEA territorial scope rule, 123
Elective eligible counterparties, 128
Elective professional clients, 127
Electronic media (COBS), 124
Electronic money, 49
Eligible counterparties, 15, 128
Eligible counterparty business, 128
Employee share schemes, 51
Encouraging (market abuse), 81
Enforcement division, 43
Enforcement manual, 45
Enhanced due diligence (EDD), 96
EU Market Abuse Directive, 80
European Economic Area (EEA), 111
Evidential provisions (Handbooks), 30
Excluded activities, 51
Excluded communications, 132
Execution only business, 136
Executive procedures, 43
Exempt persons, 41

Failure to disclose (money laundering), 88
FCA Handbook, 30
Final Notice, 43
Financial Action Task Force, 86, 100
Financial Conduct Authority (FCA), 5, 10
Financial crisis management, 9
Financial Ombudsman Service (FOS), 13, 28
Financial Policy Committee (FPC), 9
Financial promotion, 130
Financial Promotions Order, 133
Financial promotions power, 48, 132
Financial sanctions regime, 95
Financial Services and Markets Act 2000, 3
Financial Services Authority (FSA), 3

Financial Services Compensation Scheme (FSCS), 13, 28
Financial stability objective, 10
Financial stability reports (FSRs), 6
Firm Systematic Framework (FSF), 58
Firms, 13
Fit and proper, 54
Freedom of Information Act 2000, 29
Funeral plan contracts, 50, 53
Further decision notice, 44
Futures, 52

General application rule (COBS), 123
General objective (PRA), 8
General prohibition, 40
Gifts policy, 142
Guidance (status of), 30

Handbook Guides, 31
High level policy statement, 93
Home state basis (COBS), 124

Immunity notices, 79
Improper disclosure, 82
Individual Liquidity Adequacy Assessment (ILAA), 108
Inducements, 142
Industry guidance, 31
Information Commissioner, 28, 103
Injunctions, 41
Insider dealing, 77
Insider lists, 102
Insurance objective (PRA), 8
Integration (money laundering), 86
Integrity objective (FCA), 11
Interim management statement (IMS), 102
Internal audit function, 23
Internal control mechanisms, 23
Internal reconciliations (financial instruments), 152
Investment firms, 110
Investment research, 140
Investment services and activities (MiFID), 110
Investments (dealing in), 49

Joint Money Laundering Steering Group, 92

Know Your Customer (KYC), 94, 99

Large undertaking (MiFID), 127
Layering (money laundering), 86
Legal cutover (LCO), 6
Level 5 fine, 47
Liquid assets buffer, 109
Liquidity coverage ratio (LCR), 107
Listing Rules, 102
Lloyd's, 42, 50, 53

Macro-prudential policy, 5
Maintaining competence, 67
Managing investments, 50
Manipulating devices (market abuse), 82
Manipulating transactions, 82
Market abuse, 30, 80, 82
Market Abuse Directive, 147
Market makers, 78
Marketing communications, 130
Markets in Financial Instruments Directive (MiFID), 109
Misleading behaviour (market abuse), 82
Misuse of Information, 82
Mobile phones (recordings), 125
Model Code (directors' dealings), 102
Money advice service, 13
Money laundering, 24, 85
Money Laundering Directives, 86
Money Laundering Regulations 2007, 87
Money Laundering Reporting Officer, 23, 91, 97
Mortgage advice, 50
Multilateral Trading Facilities (MTFs), 16, 50, 123

N2, 49
National Crime Agency, 89, 97
National Savings & Investments, 42
Nominated Officer (money laundering), 91
Non-advised sales, 136
Non-independent research, 140
Non-statutory notices, 44

Objective test, 88
Office of Fair Trading (OFT), 27
One-off financial promotion, 132
Online Notifications and Applications (ONA), 62
Operational risk, 24
Order allocation policy, 146
Order execution policy, 145
Outcomes-focused regulation, 4, 16

Outsourcing, 24
Overall liquidity adequacy rule, 108
Overseas persons, 51

Packaged product, 131
Part 4A permission, 54, 55
Passporting, 111
Pensions mis-selling, 3
Pensions Regulator, 29
Per se eligible counterparties, 128
Per se professional clients, 126
Perimeter Guidance Manual (PERG), 31, 41
Periodic statements, 149
Personal account dealing, 147
Placement (money laundering), 86
Policy of independence, 139
Politically exposed persons (PEPs), 96
PRA Handbook, 30
Prejudicing an investigation, 90
Prescribed markets, 81
Price stabilisation, 79
Primary legislation, 29
Principles for Businesses, 14
Principles-based regulation, 4
Private Warning, 45
Proactive Intervention Framework (of PRA), 59
Proactive Intervention Framework (PIF), 8
Proceeds of Crime Act 2002, 86
Product governance, 12
Product intervention, 48
Professional clients, 126
Prohibition Order, 40, 47
Prospectus Directive, 113
Protected disclosure, 67
Protection (levels), 125
Prudential regulation, 105
Prudential Regulation Authority (PRA), 5, 8
Prudential risks, 105
Prudentially significant firms, 105
Public censure, 45
Public Interest Disclosure Act 1998, 67

Qualified investors, 113
Qualifying investment, 81

Reactive regulation, 4
Real-time financial promotion, 134
Recognised Clearing Houses (RCHs), 27, 42
Recognised Investment Exchanges (RIEs), 27, 42

INDEX

Recognised Overseas Investment Exchanges (ROIEs), 42
Record keeping, 24, 104
Record keeping (and data protection), 105
Regular market user test, 81
Regulated activities, 49
Regulated Activities Order, 49, 52
Regulated market, 81
Regulated mortgage contracts, 50, 53
Regulatory Decisions Committee, 56, 62
Regulatory Guides, 31
Reliance on others, 129
Remuneration (and conflicts of interest), 139
Remuneration Code, 25
Reporting lines, 23
Reporting lines (and conflicts of interest), 139
Repos, 53
Requiring (market abuse), 81
Resolvability (of a firm), 8
Restitution orders, 41, 46
Retail clients, 126
Retail Distribution Review (RDR), 3
Retail investment products (RIPs), 65
Risk-based approach (to regulation), 4
Rolling stock method (reconciliations), 152

Safe custody assets, 152
Safe harbours, 83, 84
Sanctions List, 95
Secondary legislation, 30
Segregation of duties, 139
Self-regulation, 3
Senior management responsibilities, 22
Serious Organised Crime and Police Act (SOCPA) 2005, 79, 88
Settlement risk, 150
Simplified due diligence (SDD), 96
Single passport (for issuers), 113
Special Resolution Unit, 8
Specialist examinations, 66
Specified investments, 52
Stakeholder pension plans, 50

Statements of misconduct, 45
Statements of Principle (for approved persons), 17
Statutory regulation, 3
Statutory trust, 151
Stress tests, 108
Student Loans Company, 42
Suitability, 134
Suitability report, 135
Supervising agencies (MLR 2007), 87
Supervisory function, 23
Supervisory Notice, 44
Switching, 148
SYSC, 90
Systemic risk, 10

TCCUT (tribunal), 29, 45
Terrorism, 98
Terrorism Act 2000, 98, 99
Third Money Laundering Directive, 86
Threshold conditions, 54
Tip sheets, 51
Tipping off (money laundering), 89
Total count method (reconciliations), 152
Trading plan, 103
Training and Competence (TC), 64
Transaction reporting, 59
Transparency Directive, 101
Treating customers fairly (TCF), 4, 16
Twin peaks regulation, 6

UCITS Directives, 112
UCITS IV, 112

Warning Notice, 43
Website conditions (COBS), 124
Whistleblowing, 67

ZEN surveillance system, 59